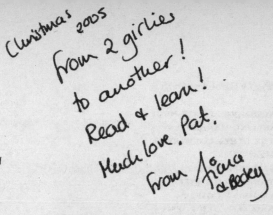

Christmas 2005
from 2 girlies
to another!
Read & learn!
Much love, Pat.
From Fiona
& Becky

OUT OF FASHION

Beats Trinny & Sussana
hands down!

Out of Fashion

an anthology of poems

edited by CAROL ANN DUFFY

faber and faber

First published in 2004
by Faber and Faber Limited
3 Queen Square London WC1N 3AU
This paperback edition first published in 2005

Photoset by RefineCatch Ltd, Bungay, Suffolk
Printed in England by Bookmarque Ltd, Croydon, Surrey

A CIP record for this book
is available from the British Library

ISBN 0–571–21995–0

10 9 8 7 6 5 4 3 2 1

Contents

VIII

Preface

One had as good be out of the world, as out of the fashion.   COLLEY CIBBER

In this anthology, I have invited over fifty of our best contemporary poets to choose a poem, by a poet from another time, which significantly concerns itself with dress or fashion. In each case, a poem by the living poet appears alongside his or her choice. A poem, if you like, is the attire of feeling: the literary form where words seem tailor-made for memory or desire. Good poems have their origins in intensely lived days or nights, yet continue to exist independently of these beginnings. Birth, work, love and death are, in themselves, messy events; but poetry is the place where they all scrub-up well.

The poems in *Out of Fashion* examine, in their different ways, how we dress or undress, how we cover up or reveal, and how clothes, fashion and jewellery are both a necessary and luxurious, a practical and sensual, a liberating and repressing part of our lives. I hope that the anthology forms an entertaining dialogue between the two arts of poetry and fashion, and between poets, men and women, from the past and present. Although the names of John Donne, Saphho, Emily Dickinson and Thomas Hardy cropped up more than once, several of the contemporary poets nominated different poems by Robert Herrick as their first choice. His perfectly-made, sensual, celebratory songs seem to strike the common note of the assembly here – the glad association in our minds between clothing and sexual or romantic love. For centuries, poets have clearly been urging their muses to get their kit off. As John Donne wrote:

Full nakedness! All joyes are due to thee,
As souls unbodied, bodies uncloth'd must be,
To taste whole joyes.

Love's opposite, in poetry, is, of course, Death, and there are many poets here who properly reflect that, from the much-loved A. E. Housman to the new poet Dorothy Molloy. The reader will find here, wearing saris and suits, scarves and stomachers, shields and shrouds, a vivid gathering of lovers, mothers, fathers, warriors and children. It is clear from these poems that, although life and art are only change, nothing really changes. The sonnet will always be the little black dress of poetry. However fashionably we dress ourselves up, we are all, in our common humanity, the same under the skin.

CAROL ANN DUFFY

CAROL ANN DUFFY

Warming Her Pearls

Next to my own skin, her pearls. My mistress
bids me wear them, warm them, until evening
when I'll brush her hair. At six, I place them
round her cool, white throat. All day I think of her,

resting in the Yellow Room, contemplating silk
or taffeta, which gown tonight? She fans herself
whilst I work willingly, my slow heat entering
each pearl. Slack on my neck, her rope.

She's beautiful. I dream about her
in my attic bed; picture her dancing
with tall men, puzzled by my faint, persistent scent
beneath her French perfume, her milky stones.

I dust her shoulders with a rabbit's foot,
watch the soft blush seep through her skin
like an indolent sigh. In her looking-glass
my red lips part as though I want to speak.

Full moon. Her carriage brings her home. I see
her every movement in my head . . . Undressing,
taking off her jewels, her slim hand reaching
for the case, slipping naked into bed, the way

she always does . . . And I lie here awake,
knowing the pearls are cooling even now
in the room where my mistress sleeps. All night
I feel their absence and I burn.

JOHN AGARD

Thirteen Ways of Looking at the Old Tie

A striped reminder
of the embers of empire.

*

A nostalgic neck-binder
for a post-colonial evening.

*

An emblem that divides
insiders from outsiders.

*

A prop for suicide
by way of strangulation.

*

An icon of Eton
worn even with the heat on.

*

A signifying signpost
to the nearest pubic station.

*

A crested spearhead
into male bonding.

*

A formal demarcator
of respect for the dead.

*

A diagonal entry
into the Royal Artillery.

*

A cross-sexual accessory
of gender-bending politics.

*

A Freudian substitute
for the umbilical cord.

*

A subliminal throwback
to the Neanderthal club.

*

In Nansi's motley wardrobe
the tie, on the other hand,

could be quite simply
a polka dot silk paddle

to row the sea of circumstance.

ANONYMOUS (Gond oral tradition)

Chosen by John Agard

My Cobra Girl

You are coming very slowly, why do you delay
    O my black cobra?
I have brought you anklets, measured to your feet
    Why do you delay, O my black cobra?

I have brought you a sari, measured to your body
    Why do you delay, O my black cobra?
I have brought you armlets, measured to your arms
    Why do you delay, O my black cobra?
You are coming very slowly, why do you delay
    O my black cobra?

MONIZA ALVI

The Sari

Inside my mother
I peered through a glass porthole.
The world beyond was hot and brown.

They were all looking in on me –
Father, Grandmother,
the cook's boy, the sweeper girl,
the bullock with the sharp
shoulder-blades,
the local politicians.

My English grandmother
took a telescope
and gazed across continents.

All the people unravelled a sari.
It stretched from Lahore to Hyderabad,
wavered across the Arabian Sea,
shot through with stars,
fluttering with sparrows and quails.
They threaded it with roads,
undulations of land.

Eventually
they wrapped and wrapped me in it
whispering *Your body is your country.*

ANONYMOUS (Japan, 8th century)

Chosen by Moniza Alvi

Poem by a Frontier Guard

While the leaves of the bamboo rustle
On a cold and frosty night,
The seven layers of clobber I wear
Are not so warm, not so warm
As the body of my wife.

Translated by Geoffrey Bownas and Anthony Thwaite

SIMON ARMITAGE

from Sir Gawain and the Green Knight

And his gear and garments were green as well:
a tight, straight coat, tailored to his shape,
and a cloak thrown over the coat, the cloth lined
with smoothly shorn fur, the outside finished off
with ermine edging and hems, as was the hood, worn
shawled on his shoulders, shucked from his head.
Lower down, his leggings were also green,
swathing his calves like green skin, and his spurs
were gold, but shimmered green with the striped silk
of his stocking feet, for this horseman was shoeless.
In all his vestment he was positively verdant!
From his belt-hooks and buckle, to the brilliant gems
worked into his saddle and stitched onto the silk –
arrayed like an aura around the man himself –
the detail of which defies proper description,
embroidered as it was with butterflies and birds
and blazoned with green beads on a background of gold.
All the horse's tack: harness pendants, hind-strap,
the eye of the bit, each alloyed and enamelled part
and the stirrups he stood in were of the same tint,
as was the saddle cantle, as were the saddle skirts,
all glimmering and glinting with green jewels.
Even the hide of the horse he rode – every hair –
          was green.
     A horse many hands high.
     The embroidered bridle strained
     when the steed snorted and shied.
     But his rider had him reined.

Chosen by Simon Armitage

from Sir Gawain and the Green Knight

Ande al grayþed in grene þis gome and his wedes:
A strayte cote ful streȝt, þat stek on his sides,
A meré mantile abof, mensked withinne
With pelure pured apert, þe pane ful clene
With blyþe blaunner ful bryȝt, and his hod boþe,
Þat watz laȝt fro his lokkez and layde on his schulderes;
Heme wel-haled hose of þat same,
Þat spenet on his sparlyr, and clene spures vnder
Of bryȝt golde, vpon silk bordes barred ful ryche,
And scholes vnder schankes þere þe schalk rides;
And alle his vesture uerayly watz clene verdure,
Boþe þe barres of his belt and oþer blyþe stones,
Þat were richely rayled in his aray clene
Aboutte hymself and his sadel, vpon silk werkez.
Þat were to tor for to telle of tryfles þe halue
Þat were enbrauded abof, wyth bryddes and flyȝes,
With gay gaudi of grene, þe golde ay inmyddes.
Þe pendauntes of his payttrure, þe proude cropure,
His molaynes, and alle þe metail anamayld was þenne,
Þe steropes þat he stod on stayned of þe same,
And his arsounz al after and his aþel skyrtes,
Þat euer glemered and glent al of grene stones;
Þe fole þat he ferkkes on fyn of þat ilke,
        sertayn,
    A grene hors gret and þikke,
    A stede ful stif to strayne,

    In brawden brydel quik—
    To þe gome he watz ful gayn.

SUJATA BHATT

In Her Green Dress, She is

In her green dress, she is
the background and the foreground –

A green dress the colour
    of iris stems,
the ones in the background –

A green dress
    the colour of iris stems against grass–

Green on green on green –

She is the foreground
    and the background –

Her face intent because
she's listening to a bird in the distance –
        a single bird – persistent –
calling again and again –
Its song slit, cleft –
            rising and falling
and rising again through the stillness.
Its song clinging to the leaves –
    A melody
that must have moved Bach –

Her face intent because irises
have flung themselves open in the heat:
Blue petals arched
like so many little blue tongues
        tasting the air –

Those yellow hearts cannot hide anymore.

Even the black stones, the oval shaped
black stones of her necklace
        can see you –

It is June: Full of humid shadows,
purple clouds – it will rain
in an hour. The irises will sway
in the wind – a few stems will
get bent by the rain – broken –
and her green dress will get drenched
    along with the grass
where the stems will lie
            broken –

But she will walk away
laughing – she will walk slowly
lingering in the green wetness –

ONO NO KOMACHI

Chosen by Sujata Bhatt

'When my desire'

When my desire
grows too fierce
I wear my bed clothes
inside out,
dark as the night's rough husk.

The Seal

Where had you been? I can't remember.
Wherever it was, you were headed for home
on Charing Cross or Tottenham Court Road
when the little silver handset tucked
in the breast pocket
of your denim jacket
took it upon itself to phone.

Hello, I said. *Hello . . . hello?*
and heard from underneath your clothes
the sound of breakers folding into foam
on shifting stones,
on a stretch of shingle,
a shore, perhaps, like this one here
where I am, at last, unreachable

a beach where the only remarkable thing
is the mottled, washed-up body of a seal
untouched as yet by any creature
and over which
someone has draped
a plastic sheet or a bin liner
like a jacket over a sleeping lover.

I might have been a concerned doctor
sitting there on our living-room floor
head inclined to a stethoscope, alert

to a hint of the
odd or irregular, listening
for what seemed like for ever
but was only, in fact, the bones of an hour.

STEVIE SMITH

Chosen by Colette Bryce

My Hat

Mother said if I wore this hat
I should be certain to get off with the right sort of chap
Well look where I am now, on a desert island
With so far as I can see no one at all on hand
I know what has happened though I suppose Mother wouldn't
  see
This hat being so strong has completely run away with me
I had the feeling it was beginning to happen the moment I put
  it on
What a moment that was as I rose up, I rose up like a flying
  swan
As strong as a swan too, why see how far my hat has flown
  me away
It took us a night to come and then a night and a day
And all the time the swan wing in my hat waved beautifully
Ah, I thought, How this hat becomes me.
First the sea was dark but then it was pale blue
And still the wing beat and we flew and we flew
A night and a day and a night, and by the old right way
Between the sun and the moon we flew until morning day.
It is always early morning here on this peculiar island
The green grass grows into the sea on the dipping land
Am I glad I am here? Yes, well, I am,
It's nice to be rid of Father, Mother and the young man
There's just one thing causes me a twinge of pain,
If I take my hat off, shall I find myself home again?
So in this early morning land I always wear my hat
Go home, you see, well I wouldn't run a risk like that.

15

Dance

Dressed in blue, I could
turn in the wind,
insert myself gently
into immediate matter.

Dressed in green, I could
provoke a disaster
that would never have happened
dressed in alabaster.

Dressed in red, I could
trace a diagonal
from one shore to the other – well done! –
to help pass a diaphonous army.

Dressed in yellow, I could slide
to death's side
– and so on.

W. B. YEATS

Chosen by Nina Cassian

A Coat

I made my song a coat
Covered with embroideries
Out of old mythologies
From heel to throat;
But the fools caught it,
Wore it in the world's eyes
As though they'd wrought it.
Song, let them take it
For there's more enterprise
In walking naked.

My Father Had Two Coats

I didn't exactly take it off him
while his body was still warm.
No, it wasn't like that at all,
though I did eye it up in the closet
for weeks before he died –
in fact for months and years.

It was an up-town coat;
charcoal cashmere herringbone, outside
and inside, silk with secret pockets hidden
in the lining. The buttons at the cuff
popped up through slitted button holes.
Look how they open and close and let the
cuffs turn up in such a perky way. It's easy
to imagine the business trends he followed
Monday to Friday in the *New York Times*,
Long Island Rail Road, Port Washington line.

This coat said everything. Now,
when I wear it, it talks to me
and keeps me warm.

In fact, much later, when I saw him
swaddled in white plastic, the kind
you couldn't see through at all,
though it was opened at the neck
and bunched behind his head as
if it were a hood, he was cold.

In places the plastic was taped,
in others, it was tucked like a careless
sheet in a down-town rooming house.
His eyes were closed and his jaw
was wrapped to keep his mouth in place.
How light-weight the covering was,
so like the packaging we use to
bundle up the stuff we throw away.
Just a thin film keeping it all together.

This coat said everything.
It clings to me. I listen.
I'm cold.

ANONYMOUS

Chosen by Linda Chase

Madrigal

My Love in her attire doth show her wit,
    It doth so well become her;
For every season she hath dressings fit,
    For Winter, Spring, and Summer.
No beauty she doth miss
When all her robes are on;
But Beauty's self she is
When all her robes are gone.

KATE CLANCHY

Long Boots,

with hooks,
are in this year.
Some look to take an hour
or more to criss cross precisely
from the foot, to loop,
tighten, tug the yard
of hard-gripped
cord. And

to untie,
peel slowly from
each thigh, each calf,
wrench off leather where it grips
tighter round the heel, the instep, over
the twitching nose of toes,
takes, I'd say, a mirror,
certain music,
days.

I like
their icy, skateboot
strangeness. That girl
for instance – watch her inch
to the edge of her perch, unconscious,
lost, to herself, to us,
in her marvellous
alien
legs.

PHILIP LARKIN

Chosen by Kate Clanchy

The Large Cool Store

The large cool store selling cheap clothes
Set out in simple sizes plainly
(Knitwear, Summer Casuals, Hose,
In browns and greys, maroon and navy)
Conjures the weekday world of those

Who leave at dawn low terraced houses
Timed for factory, yard and site.
But past the heaps of shirts and trousers
Spread the stands of Modes For Night:
Machine-embroidered, thin as blouses,

Lemon, sapphire, moss-green, rose
Bri-Nylon Baby-Dolls and Shorties
Flounce in clusters. To suppose
They share that world, to think their sort is
Matched by something in it, shows

How separate and unearthly love is,
Or women are, or what they do,
Or in our young unreal wishes
Seem to be: synthetic, new,
And natureless in ecstasies.

Amber

Coveted week after week on the market stall,
coiled, nonchalant, arrayed under the lid
of locked glass, they grew familiar.
She'd finger them, slip them over her head,
try them for size, spoilt for choice –
red-amber, yellow, cut Russian ruby,
or those sad rosaries, widow's beads of Whitby jet.
In each bead surfaced the cloudy face of a woman.

Warmed by the sunlight on dressing tables,
or against a woman's skin, then laid safe
in a drawer each night between the silk leaves
of her underwear. Never cold, as if
each bead were the unquenchable flame
that burned a million years like a sanctuary lamp
beneath the ice, each drip of sticky gold
hardening to honeyed gold.

As if nothing that has ever contained heat
can be cold again, mirrors never empty
and our rooms, furniture, hoarded amulets,
could reassemble themselves into a life
and still pass hand to hand from underneath
the permafrost, ice woman to living daughter.

ANONYMOUS (16th century)

Chosen by Gillian Clarke

The Shirt of a Lad

As I did the washing one day
Under the bridge at Aberteifi,
And a golden stick to drub it,
And my sweetheart's shirt beneath it –
A knight came by upon a charger,
Proud and swift and broad of shoulder,
And he asked if I would sell
The shirt of the lad that I loved well.

No, I said, I will not trade –
Not if a hundred pounds were paid;
Not if two hillsides I could keep
Full with wethers and white sheep;
Not if two fields full of oxen
Under yoke were in the bargain;
Not if the herbs of all Llanddewi,
Trodden and pressed, were offered to me –
Not for the likes of that, I'd sell
The shirt of the lad that I love well.

Translated from Welsh by Anthony Conran

24

The World's Biggest Suit

Lapels on my three-piece suit no broader than a nose bridge,
Stripes, bellbottoms, turn-ups, buttonhole smiling for a rose,
Waistcoat of hemp or mail, fob watch looped on a chain.
Trilby, not a Stetson, thrown on a hook three feet away,
Or twirled on my index finger, a necktie loose enough to show
I have a neck to speak of, top button open to free my Adam's
    apple.

That's me in a rendition of a scream not because my Apple
Stalls with pop-ups, but as I join James Brown on his bridge.
When I step out of all that finery it's like I want to show
Me how I can diss myself – When is a rose not a rose?
When it is a Rorschach of me against me – by walking away
Into transparency: Ellison's invisibility; Equiano's ball and
    chain.

My suit takes my name, my gait, to wake on the right side, a
    chain
Reaction I could go on with, and think I will, now that the
    apple,
Rotten to the core, misses more than one bite. For I cannot
    take away
My night time from my right time, when heels click tarmac to
    bridge
The gap between the sound of me and my arrival, or when my
    rose
Aftershave turns the corner ahead of me and heads swerve to
    see the show.

If I sleep in my suit it's like I never went to bed but stayed up
   to show
The party people how to really party: until liquor runs out and
   the chain
Of suits waiting for the loo breaks and heads for behind the
   rose
Bushes – stoop and raise skirt, unzip aim and fire at the base
   of the apple
Tree – then back to raiding cupboards just to limbo under the
   bridge
Of sobriety with anything that remotely resembles the
   fermented, a way

To keep the demons at arms length. Buttons undone,
   thingamabob put away
But flies not fully zipped, reefer ash on my sleeves, and, if
   lucky, the show
But don't tell chartreuse lipstick on my cream collar. Oh planet
   of bridge
Players and those who do not partake, answer this, your
   history tries to chain
Me and I serve a little Timex strapped to my wrist, but what if
   the only apple
In history were Newton's and there was no garden seeded with
   mortality's rose?

Then I would be a suit. No more, no less, Fingers stink with
   the rose
Of a finger job, lips numb from snogging. Flies shut, shop
   shuttered away
For the night. Not the same suit, never the same suit twice, in
   an apple
Orchard of such suits, oh Zen of the sartorial! My heart on
   show

On my sleeve, my soul in the heel of my rap and tap leather
    strap and chain
Link foot wrap, sparks on the dance floor as I find the funky
    bridge.

To the cantilevered rose in my thighs and xylophone caged
    away in my ribs;
To my spine, a cored apple, the maracas in my hungry belly
    show
And my skin's chain-stitched three-piece suit; to the bridge!

Chosen by Fred d'Aguiar

from Canterbury Tales

A good WIF was ther OF biside BATHE,
But she was somdel deef, and that was scathe.
Of clooth-makyng she hadde swich an haunt
She passed hem of Ypres and of Gaunt.
In al the parisshe wif ne was ther noon
That to the offrynge bifore hire sholde goon;
And if ther dide, certeyn so wrooth was she
That she was out of alle charitee.
Hir coverchiefs ful fyne weren of ground;
I dorste swere they weyeden ten pound
That on a Sonday weren upon hir heed.
Hir hosen weren of fyn scarlet reed,
Ful streite yteyd, and shoes ful moyste and newe.
Boold was hir face, and fair, and reed of hewe.
She was a worthy womman al hir lyve:
Housbondes at chirche dore she hadde fyve,
Withouten oother compaignye in youthe –
But therof nedeth nat to speke as nowthe.
And thries hadde she been at Jerusalem;
She hadde passed many a straunge strem;
At Rome she hadde been, and at Boloigne,
In Galice at Seint-Jame, and at Coloigne.
She koude muchel of wandrynge by the weye.
Gat-tothed was she, soothly for to seye.
Upon an amblere esily she sat,
Ywympled wel, and on hir heed an hat
As brood as is a bokeler or a targe;
A foot-mantel aboute hir hipes large,

And on hir feet a paire of spores sharpe.
In felaweshipe wel koude she laughe and carpe.
Of remedies of love she knew per chaunce,
For she koude of that art the olde daunce.

somdel deef, *somewhat deaf;* that was scathe, *that was a pity;* haunt, *skill;*
Ypres, Gaunt, *Ypres, Ghent, cloth-making centres in modern Belgium;*
offrynge, *offering (when people go to the altar with their offerings at Mass);*
wrooth, *angry;* out of alle charitee, *deeply upset;* coverchiefs, *linen coverings
for the head;* fyne weren of ground, *were fine in texture;* dorste swere, *dare
swear;* weyeden, *weighed;* hosen, *stockings;* streite yteyd, *closely laced;*
moyste, *supple;* chirche door, *door of the church;* withouten, *not counting;* as
nowthe, *now;* Jerusalem, Rome, Boloigne, (Boulogne in France), in Galice at
Seint-Jame (St James of Compostella in Galicia, Spain), and Coloigne
(Cologne) *were celebrated places of pilgrimage;* straunge strem, *foreign sea;*
Gat-tothed, *with teeth set wide apart;* amblere, *a pacing horse;* esily,
comfortably; Ywympled wel, *wearing a large wimple, a head dress that covers
all but the face;* brood as is a bokeler or a targe, *broad as a buckler or shield;*
foot-mantel, *an apron-like overskirt;* spores, *spurs;* carpe, *chatter;* remedies of
love, *remedies for love-sickness;* per chaunce, *as it happened;* olde daunce,
tricks of the trade, game of love

Maroon

That year I wore maroon, hid
in the attic, by bulbous lamps

darkly cloaked in aubergine,
grew my fringe, shut out the light,

gorged on it, in caftans, shawls, soaked
in red wine, smoked Passing Clouds.

It seemed so hip, so dank, so blurred,
I drifted, hardly breathed or spoke

to them downstairs, all red and white,
with their cornflakes, tablecloths.

Mother gripped the banister
and called to me through purple fog

Come down, she crooned, *I've ironed a shirt
Come down, walk on my hoovered floors!*

But I lingered in my night lagoon,
cocooned in drapes, I never looked

underneath, I never bathed,
and I grew ripe, yeasty, strong.

It was a shock when I emerged,
flapping, into white daylight.

ROBERT BURNS

Chosen by Julia Darling

To a Louse

On Seeing one on a Lady's Bonnet at Church

Ha! whare ye gaun, ye crowlin ferlie!
Your impudence protects you sairly:
I canna say but ye strunt rarely,
  Owre gauze and lace;
Tho' faith, I fear ye dine but sparely,
  On sic a place.

Ye ugly, creepan, blastet wonner,
Detested, shunn'd, by saunt an' sinner,
How daur ye set your fit upon her,
  Sae fine a lady!
Gae somewhere else and seek your dinner,
  On some poor body.

Swith, in some beggar's haffet squattle,
There ye may creep, and sprawl, and sprattle,
Wi' ither kindred, jumping cattle,
  In shoals and nations;
Whare horn nor bane ne'er daur unsettle,
  Your thick plantations.

Now haud ye there, ye're out o' sight,
Below the fatt'rels, snug and tight,
Na faith ye yet! ye'll no be right,
  Till ye've got on it,
The vera tapmost, towering height
  O' Miss's bonnet.

My sooth! right bauld ye set your nose out,
As plump an' grey as onie grozet:
O for some rank, mercurial rozet,
        Or fell, red smeddum,
I'd gie ye sic a hearty dose o't,
        Wad dress your droddum!

I wad na been surpriz'd to spy
You on an auld wife's flainen toy;
Or aiblins some bit duddie boy,
        On's wylecoat;
But Miss's fine Lunardi! – fie!
        How daur ye do't?

O Jenny, dinna toss your head,
An' set your beauties a' abread!
Ye little ken what cursed speed
        The blastie's makin!
Thae winks and finger-ends, I dread,
        Are notice takin!

O wad some Power the giftie gie us
To see oursels as others see us!
It wad frae monie a blunder free us
        An' foolish notion:
What airs in dress an' gait wad lea'e us,
        And ev'n Devotion!

Sari

The street stretches its back.
Its spine cracks with satisfaction.

There's no bustle, no sense of rush,
just the determined slip and slap
of soap on slate
and cloth on stone,
morning light thrashed out
on the wet step
above the water-tank.

Her arm an arc, her haunch
pushed back,
the whole length of sari
thwacked.
Legs apart, she attacks
the sweat of yesterday,
the cooking smells,
the dribble from the baby's mouth,
drives them out
of thin and daily thinning cloth.

Today she wears the purple,
washes green,
tosses it out to dry,
smacks it down across the stones
like an accomplishment
of fine clean weave.

Sun and light shine through.
Through and through,
the day begun.

The city rolls its hip,
picks up its plastic bucket,
walks away.

ANONYMOUS (Tamil)

Chosen by Imtiaz Dharker

What Her Friend Said

But look,

look at him out there

standing like a sentinel
who keeps a rain-tank from flooding,

> rain-wet bright sword
> hung at his side,
> war anklet
> twined with moss,
> his striped waist-cloth
> tight,
> and wet with dew.

Translated by A. K. Ramanujan

MAURA DOOLEY

La Rebeca

The girl who gave her name to a Spanish cardigan,
giving not her own name but that of a ghost
looks back, beyond Menabilly, to the idea of a past.
She's no one you could name, this slight and dowdy girl,
the girl who would one day give another's name to a cardigan,
the girl so certain sure in the end of love, of mutability,
of the swan within, that all the ladies of Spain as one
threw off their shawls and wrapped their lovely breasts
in lambswool, cashmere, a row of seed pearl buttons.
That girl looks back, past Manderley, to the idea of a future,
railings, the war, but then another war and the next,
to this woman, now, breath held at the sight of a coal black,
crepe suit, french seamed, an exquisite cut. Try it,
the shop voice says, and she does. It isn't really me.
So in her shadowy closet, like a fire banked for the night,
it waits, for the moment when that woman decides for a
    second time,
not to be herself. Then the fire will spark up
and the ashes will blow towards us, blow towards us,
with the salt wind from the sea.

CHRISTOPHER MARLOWE

Chosen by Maura Dooley

The Passionate Shepherd to his Love

Come live with me, and be my love,
And we will all the pleasures prove,
That valleys, groves, hills and fields,
Woods, or steepy mountain yields.

And we will sit upon the rocks,
Seeing the shepherds feed their flocks
By shallow rivers, to whose falls
Melodious birds sing madrigals.

And I will make thee beds of roses,
And a thousand fragrant posics,
A cap of flowers and a kirtle
Embroidered all with leaves of myrtle.

A gown made of the finest wool
Which from our pretty lambs we pull,
Fair lined slippers for the cold,
With buckles of the purest gold;

A belt of straw and ivy-buds,
With coral clasps and amber studs,
And if these pleasures may thee move,
Come live with me, and be my love.

The shepherd swains shall dance and sing
For thy delight each May morning,
If these delights thy mind may move,
Then live with me, and be my love.

Grave Goods

Your sheepskin coat   purse in the pocket
Hong Kong dragon   on a silk jacket

Charm bracelet   locket heart
The faithful dog   Ship of Good Hope

A cupid bow   time's silver arrow
These twenty-five years   exactly tonight

71,725 days   1,721,400 hours
Too many to thread   to hold or tell

So what should I leave   as counters or measures –
Grey pebbles for years   green coins for days

And for the winter's   tale of eternity
A pair of slippers   my childish gift

Of suede and wool   like the Egyptian lady's
3000 years in the tomb   and still prêt à porter

A. E. HOUSMAN

Chosen by Nick Drake

from Last Poems (xx)

The night is freezing fast,
    To-morrow comes December;
        And winterfalls of old
Are with me from the past;
    And chiefly I remember
        How Dick would hate the cold.

Fall, winter, fall; for he,
    Prompt hand and headpiece clever,
        Has woven a winter robe,
And made of earth and sea
    His overcoat for ever,
        And wears the turning globe.

DOUGLAS DUNN

Empty Wardrobes

I sat in a dress shop, trying to look
As dapper as a young ambassador
Or someone who'd impressed me in a book,
A literary rake or movie star.

Clothes are a way of exercising love.
False? A little. And did she like it? Yes.
Days, days, romantic as Rachmaninov,
A ploy of style, and now not comfortless.

She walked out from the changing-room in brown,
A pretty smock with its embroidered fruit;
Dress after dress, a lady-like red gown
In which she flounced, a smart career-girl's suit.

The dress she chose was green. She found it in
Our clothes-filled cabin trunk. The pot-pourri,
In muslin bags, was full of where and when.
I turn that scent like a memorial key.

But there's that day in Paris, that I regret,
When I said No, franc-less and husbandly.
She browsed through hangers in the Lafayette,
And that comes back tonight, to trouble me.

Now there is grief the couturier, and grief
The needlewoman mourning with her hands,
And grief the scattered finery of life,
The clothes she gave as keepsakes to her friends.

JAY LIVINGSTON AND RAY EVANS

Chosen by Douglas Dunn

Buttons and Bows

East is east and west is west
And the wrong one I have chose
Let's go where they keep on wearin'
Those frills and flowers and buttons and bows
Rings and things and buttons and bows.

Don't bury me in this prairie
Take me where the cement grows
Let's move down to some big town
Where they love a gal by the cut o' her clothes
And you'll stand out, In buttons and bows.

I'll love you in buckskin
Or skirts that you've homespun
But I'll love ya' longer, stronger where
Yer friends don't tote a gun

My bones denounce the buckboard bounce
And the cactus hurts my toes
Let's vamoose where gals keep a-usin'
Those silks and satins and linen that shows
And I'm all yours in buttons and bows.

Gimme eastern trimmin' where women are women
In high silk hose and peek-a-boo clothes
And French perfume that rocks the room
And I'm all yours in buttons and bows.

Nothing but Curves
(having read about the underwear industry)

I

How wonderful the courtesan clothes
of our imagination. Diaphanous, flowing, they droop
over heavy counterpanes at the foot of the bed.

Having unlaced the memory
of grandmother's corsets blushing at me
– hanging ribs, like a human abattoir –

silky girls come to mind:
sliding in on memory's watercoloured canvas
– frameless, without hook or eye to hold them,

or a flannel hairshirt to flay and squeeze them,
no underwire to uplift them
to yet-unfettered heights.

The breast is the golden globe, whispering suggestions
to ruffled organza drifts,
serenely lanolined liberty bodices.

These things are full of calm,
their frail ribbons liberate
the motherland of the self,

making country a homeland all to herself:
where a woman is free of her pressure;
her self a blank sheet between her own hands.

2

– but by fluorescent light – this is hydraulics,
refined by forensic scientists, cantilevering
their brand-new way of getting

the rounded breast into bed. This is a lode to be mined:
thirty sections origami together
to create the other, the perfect orb.

Look. And you'll see that the stars of the screen
lie when they say they have hidden secrets:
their breasts push their facelifts up to their chins

and the body politic spurs on the scuba divers
as they bounce the buoys down in the bay.
There's no future these days in swimming alone.

3

'Nothing but curves' crows the ad –
but I return, barefoot, to the dark ages
to peer at a woman who stands in half-darkness

opening a hook and eye,
placing them in a drawer where they won't be disturbed
before slipping out of her soft fleece

by the candle's eye. Climbing the mattress
she slips into her fold, closing
with a 'good night' the gap
between herself and the bottomless pit
by sleeping on her front with scripture in mind,

putting tongue and flesh safe by for a while.

The night is a sinless sarcophagus –
rasping, hard like a blind man's kiss.

Translated from the Welsh by Elin ap Hywee

Chosen by Menna Elfyn

Song to a Child

Dinogad's smock is pied, pied –
Made it out of marten hide.
Whit, whit, whistle along,
Eight slaves with you sing the song.

When your dad went to hunt,
Spear on his shoulder, cudgel in hand,
He called his quick dogs, 'Giff, you wretch,
Gaff, catch her, catch her, fetch, fetch!'

From a coracle he'd spear
Fish as a lion strikes a deer.
When your dad went to the crag
He brought down roebuck, boar and stag,
Speckled grouse from the mountain tall,
Fish from Derwent waterfall.

Whatever your dad found with his spear,
Boar or wild cat, fox or deer,
Unless it flew, would never get clear.

Translated from the Welsh by Tony Conran

U. A. FANTHORPE

Rag Trade
for Diana Hendry

Winter is exclusive. Such shape-defining whiteness
Can be worn only by the fine-boned, the unsoiled.

Spring is proverbially cruel. That special yellow
Kills all but the most invincible complexions.

And the variations on green that summer
Unendingly designs. Redheads alone can live with them.

But autumn, with her Blood-and-Bile range,
Her crepy textures. We all gravitate to her house.

BEN JONSON

Chosen by U. A. Fanthorpe

'Still to be neat'

Still to be neat, still to be dressed,
As you were going to a feast;
Still to be powdered, still perfumed:
Lady, it is to be presumed,
Though art's hid causes are not found,
All is not sweet, all is not sound.

Give me a look, give me a face,
That makes simplicity a grace;
Robes loosely flowing, hair as free:
Such sweet neglect more taketh me
Than all the adulteries of art;
They strike mine eyes, but not my heart.

The Gift

I see her in the street
and pull a gun out of my handbag.

That's in a dream.

Awake, I'm Medea:
imagining my husband's
Greek princess unwrapping
my gift of a wedding dress.

She slips it over her head:
twirling in the mirror, pouting,
swinging her hips, pushing out
her breasts.
                    Still happy,
still thinking, *he loves me*,
nothing can ever go wrong;
and loving him more, like meat with salt,
for the wife and children he's left,
she discovers the crown,
its filigree of gold leaves
trembling and tinkling
as she lifts it onto her head.

                    Then an itch
on her shoulder, and her finger
under the strap, scratching,
making it worse; and a prickling
in her hair, as if she's got lice –
but lice with the teeth of bats;

then on belly and buttocks and back
a stinging like rolling in nettles;
and then everywhere the dress
and crown touch, her flesh burning –
so she's twisting and leaping,
the cool girl he prefers
to his fiery wife, dripping
flame and shrieking.

ANNE SEXTON

Chosen by Vicki Feaver

Woman with Girdle

Your midriff sags toward your knees;
your breasts lie down in air,
their nipples as uninvolved
as warm starfish.
You stand in your elastic case,
still not giving up the new-born
and the old-born cycle.
Moving, you roll down the garment,
down that pink snapper and hoarder,
as your belly, soft as pudding,
slops into the empty space;
down, over the surgeon's careful mark,
down over hips, those head cushions
and mouth cushions,
slow motion like a rolling pin,
over crisp hairs, that amazing field
that hides your genius from your patron;
over thighs, thick as young pigs,
over knees like saucers,
over calves, polished as leather,
down toward the feet.
You pause for a moment,
tying your ankles into knots.
Now you rise,
a city from the sea,
born long before Alexandria was,
straightway from God you have come
into your redeeming skin.

49

ROGER GARFITT

Waiting for the Day

Plimsoles takes the floor. Blossoms as the Bar
whoops and whistles. As if he were
treading water, as if rough music were the water
where a strange nature uncurls and flowers,
he slow-motions to the door. Already in replay,
an old clip run and re-run, his white hipsters
step and flare. His white raincoat
capes and swirls. He is all woman.
We are all eyes.

Sullen, in black, his fetch
steps tersely at his side.

Shanghai? Marseilles? Tilbury.
Last light over warehouse roofs.
Darkness asphalts the waste ground.

Not a sound when he re-enters.
Buys an armful of beer cans. Outside,
hurls them one by one against the wall,

repeatedly. Gathers them up, shoulders
hunched in the white T-shirt.
Cradles them back to the ship.

We nurse our halves. Tomorrow
if a crew is short – someone
fails to report – one of us
will get a ship. On completion
of the trip, union papers.

St James Infirmary Blues

I went down to St James Infirmary
To see my baby there,
She was lyin' on a long white table,
So sweet, so cool, so fair.

Went up to see the doctor,
'She's very low,' he said,
Went back to see my baby
Good God! She's lying there dead.

I went down to old Joe's barroom,
On the corner by the square.
They were serving drinks as usual,
And the usual crowd was there.

On my left stood old Joe McKennedy,
And his eyes were bloodshot red;
He turned to the crowd around him,
These are the words he said:

Let her go, let her go, God bless her;
Wherever she may be,
She may search the wide world over
And never find a better man than me.

Oh, when I die, please bury me
In my ten dollar Stetson hat;
Put a twenty-dollar gold piece on my watch chain
So my friends'll know I died standin' pat.

Get six gamblers to carry my coffin
Six chorus girls to sing me a song
Put a twenty-piece jazz band on my tail gate
To raise Hell as we go along.

Now that's the end of my story
Let's have another round of booze
And if anyone should ask you just tell them
I've got the St James Infirmary blues.

ANN GRAY

Twice

The mirror holds me. So do you.
My long black coat hangs open,
my hat, my bag, my gloves
are thrown across your floor.

Outside, the boats are in,
lorries rumble past,
voices call and shout,
footsteps tap along the pavement.

I watch you twice, sixteen fingers
unlacing thin black ribbon,
four hands, four breasts.
I am breathing fast enough

for both of me.
You are behind me twice,
everywhere at once.
The day is folding.

THOMAS HARDY

Chosen by Ann Gray

A Gentleman's Second-hand Suit

Here it is hanging in the sun
    By the pawn-shop door,
A dress-suit – all its revels done
    Of heretofore.
Long drilled to the waltzers' swing and sway,
    As its tokens show:
What it has seen, what it could say
    If it did but know!

The sleeve bears still a print of powder
    Rubbed from her arms
When she warmed up as the notes swelled louder
    And livened her charms –

Or rather theirs, for beauties many
    Leant there, no doubt,
Leaving these tell-tale traces when he
    Spun them about.

Its cut seems rather in bygone style
    On looking close,
So it mayn't have bent it for some while
    To the dancing pose:
Anyhow, often within its clasp
    Fair partners hung,
Assenting to the wearer's grasp
    With soft sweet tongue.

Where is, alas, the gentleman
    Who wore this suit?

And where are his ladies? Tell none can:
    Gossip is mute.
Some of them may forget him quite
    Who smudged his sleeve,
Some think of a wild and whirling night
    With him, and grieve.

Camel Hair

Every few years it becomes
a question of backbone.

Anhedonia,
not love of winter

but a loss of the feel of the world,
a way ahead of the cold.

Even the cells refuse
to talk to one another.

As black and white
as a two-hour wait on the kerb

of a six-lane arterial road,
in a secondhand straw-coloured Dior coat,

for the last bus and its overload
to accelerate past out of its own

well-oiled backsplash.

ELIZABETH BISHOP

Chosen by Lavinia Greenlaw

Exchanging Hats

Unfunny uncles who insist
in trying on a lady's hat,
– oh, even if the joke falls flat,
we share your slight transvestite twist

in spite of our embarrassment.
Costume and custom are complex.
The headgear of the other sex
inspires us to experiment.

Anandrous aunts, who, at the beach
with paper plates upon your laps,
keep putting on the yachtsmen's caps
with exhibitionistic screech,

the visors hanging o'er the ear
so that the golden anchors drag,
– the tides of fashion never lag.
Such caps may not be worn next year.

Or you who don the paper plate
itself, and put some grapes upon it,
or sport the Indian's feather bonnet,
– perversities may aggravate

the natural madness of the hatter.
And if the opera hats collapse
and crowns grow draughty, then, perhaps,
he thinks what might a miter matter?

Unfunny uncle, you who wore a
hat too big, or one too many,
tell us, can't you, are there any
stars inside your black fedora?

Aunt exemplary and slim,
with avernal eyes, we wonder
what slow changes they see under
their vast, shady, turned-down brim.

The Beautiful Boots

for Dorothy's DMs

Navvy boots
Christmas-caked, clotted
with ochre, greensand, rust, fool's gold . . .

Reptile boots
that slough scales of paint
on the carpet, new-hatched, Cretaceously old . . .

Boot boulders
speckled with bird-droppings,
blue-, black- and snow-berry, yellow chanterelles . . .

Boot icons
gilt-crusted, tarnished
and blunt as the cudgels of Byzantine bells . . .

Battle boots
fresh from kicking the daylights
out of rainbows . . . Boots stamping their ground . . .

Boot shrines
woozy with sock incense . . .
Chariots of feet that refuse to be bound

but are bound for somewhere . . . Boots to scuff
and spatter up the mud we're stuck in,
kid . . . Walk on.

Chosen by Philip Gross

from Sir Gawain and the Green Knight

She handed him a rich ring, worked in reddish gold,
With one bright stone, standing alone,
That blazed and sparkled, brilliant as the burning sun;
Oh, I warrant it was worth a rich man's wealth.
But the knight refused it and fair and free he spoke:
'I want no gracious gifts, lady, at this time;
I have none to tender you, and none will I take.'
Still she urged insistently, and still he refused her
And swore by his sooth that he would not accept it.
Then, grieved that he denied her, she sighed and declared:
'Though you refuse my ring because it seems too rich,
You would not be beholden so highly unto me
If I gave you my girdle; that would obligate you less.'
She lightly loosed a lace that was looped around her waist,
Knit upon her kirtle beneath the clear mantle –
This girdle was of green silk, trimmed in goodly gold,
Fairly braided round about by fine and cunning fingers;
And that she gave to Gawain and goodly she besought him
To take and accept it, unworthy though it be.
But still he was steadfast and swore he could never
Accept gold or gifts before God sent him grace
Boldly to achieve the chance he had chosen there.
'And therefore I pray you, do not be displeased,
But peace to your pleadings and your importunings
         True and free.
     I am beholden to you,
     And ever will be;
     What service I can do you,
     Demand it of me.'

'Now you forsake this silk,' said the lady slyly,
'Because it's simple in itself, as indeed it seems;
Lo! it is so little, and even less its worth,
But he who knows the virtues woven deep within it,
He would, perhaps, put a higher price upon it,
For whosoever girds himself with this green girdle,
While he has it neatly hasped around his waist
Nothing under Heaven can hew him down or harm him,
For not by any force or sleight may he be hurt or slain.'
Then the knight considered, and it came into his heart
That this might stand him in good stead when he stood his
    stroke
At the wild chapel where his foe awaited;
Might he escape unslain, the sleight would be worthy.
Then he listened silently and suffered her to speak,
And she pressed it upon him and urged him to accept,
And he granted, and she gave it with a good will
And begged and besought him never to betray her,
But to hide it from her husband, and he agreed
That none would ever know of it but those two alone,
     For any price.
    He thanked her, and then
    She who had kissed him twice
    Embraced him once again,
    And now has kissed him thrice.

Translated from the Middle English by James L. Rosenberg

DAVID HARSENT

from Marriage

Now rise from the bath, your hair caught up with a peg.
The water peels back from your breasts like the film from a
    cooking egg.
You cleanly cleave your arse as you lift one leg

to the edge of the tub and start to work the towel
from ankle to thigh, then into the dark bevel
of your crotch, after which you sit, heel to knee,

on a raffia chair, your quim guerning to a scowl
as you slip your foot into the foot
of your stocking. Next, it's your face coming free

of the summer dress, as you greet
yourself in the mirror. Here's how it goes after that:
    foundation, powder, eye-
shadow, blusher, mascara,

lipstick pressed to a tissue . . . that perfectly mute
syllable of love (love, or it could be hate)
that I pick up and pocket to re-read later.

The same summer dress you loosened and dropped with a
    clatter
of tiny buttons on tile as I backed you up to the table,
our first night under this roof, and you The Biddable

Spouse, slipping your foot out of the foot
of your stocking . . . The same table
you cover with a red checkered cloth, setting the bread, the
    butter,

the plum preserve, and the best we have of china.
Ur-wife. Wife of wives.
I'm close enough for ambush as you pass with your box of
knives.

ROBERT HERRICK

Chosen by David Harsent

Delight in Disorder

A sweet disorder in the dresse
Kindles in cloathes a wantonnesse:
A Lawne about the shoulders thrown
Into a fine distraction:
An erring Lace, which here and there
Enthralls the Crimson Stomacher:
A Cuffe neglectful, and thereby
Ribbands to flow confusedly:
A winning wave (deserving Note)
In the tempestuous petticote:
A carelesse shooe-string, in whose tye
I see a wilde civility:
Doe more bewitch me, then when Art
Is too precise in every part.

DAVID HART

I Thought I'd Wear

I thought I'd wear the most sparkling sea I could find
so I travelled the coasts and waited for that bright light
and waited for that relaxed roll of the waves
and for that turn of the tide into the sun's striptease fire,

and when the moment came I jumped
and swam fast and far out,
and I called to the people walking the beach
but no-one saw me,
and I waved to the people walking the beach
but no one saw me,

and I shouted to the people with their cameras
but no one saw me,
and I opened my arms to the people with their cameras
but no one collected me.

Now I walk in grey,
I want to know what is greyer than grey
so that at the edge of the sea
I can wear it.

Chosen by David Hart

The Beau's Receipt for a Lady's Dress

Hang a small bugle cap on, as big as a crown,
Snout it off with a flow'r. vulgo dict, a Pompoun,
Let your powder be gay, and braid up your hair,
Like the mane of a colt to be sold at a Fair.
Like the mane etc.

A short pair of jumps, half an ell from your chin,
To make you appear as one just lying-in;
Before your brest pin a stomacher bib on,
Ragout it with curlets of silver and ribbon.

Your neck and your shoulders both naked should be,
A-la-mode de Vandyke, bloun with chevaux de frize,
Let your goun be a sack, blue, yellow or green,
And frizzle your elbous with ruffles sixteen.

Furl off your lawn apron with flounces in rows,
Puff and pucker up knots on your arms and your toes,
Make your petticoats short, that a hoop 8 yards wide
May decently shew how your garters are ty'd.

With fringes of knotting your dicky cabob,
On slippers of velvet set gold a-la-daube;
But mount on French heels when you go to a ball,
'Tis the fashion to totter, and show you can fall.
Throw modesty out from your manners and face,
A la-mode de francois, you're a bit for his grace.

Shirt

When I go outside in the autumn night
to fetch in washing that's almost dried
in the still mild air – and it's mostly my sons' T-shirts
and shirts, and they're mostly pale,
blue or white, I see how they hang
loose from the hem, how the empty sleeves
and cuffs just stir when I fill my arms
how they flop over the crook of my elbow
– and they're soft now and cool,
and I think how they'll open and swell
with the different shapes of my sons,
how even now those shapes are there
(how I can tell in the dark which shirt is which)
how they keep the scent of their flesh and sweat
under the astringent soapy smell; and when they're dressed
in those shirts and the cloth is close to the skin
how I can see their chests lift and depress,
the older son's narrow concave chest –
the way his ribs project – the younger
one taller and broader now. And I don't like to throw
a shirt away, even when it's worn so thin, the ribbed
side seams and welt have unstitched,
and it's rubbed so soft the dark blots of ink
and grease have washed in, become part of the cloth.
And I rub my fingers over the pearly nubs
of buttons, over the frayed collar and cuffs,
then I take off the buttons and keep the rest
for shoe cloths and dust cloths. But before

I do with these shirts I bring in, that fall and flop
and wind themselves round and over my arms
the way my sons' real bodies don't anymore –
I slide a hand inside each one
as if I could find, like those Russian dolls
the smaller school shirts, sports shirts, T-shirts,
vests, the little cap sleeves and stretchy envelope necks,
the silky stitched hems; how it seems no more
from that time to this mild autumn, than it does from now
to the season ahead, when I'll go outside in the winter night
and prise off the line the same washed shirts
that are cold and white and stiff with frost.

SAPPHO

Chosen by Jo Haslam

'Don't ask me what to wear'

Don't ask me what to wear
I have no embroidered
headband from Sardis to
give you, Cleis, such as
I wore
      and my mother
always said that in her
day a purple ribbon
looped in the hair was thought
to be high style indeed

but we were dark:
           a girl
whose hair is yellower than
torchlight should wear no
headdress but fresh flowers

Translated from the Greek by Mary Barnard

RITA ANN HIGGINS

Remapping the Borders

In Texas
after the conference
they put on a céilí,
nearly everyone danced,
a few of us Margarita'd.

In jig time
everyone knew everyone.
After the Siege of Ennis
a woman asked me,
'Could you see my stocking belt
as I did the swing?'

I was taken aback.

Me, thigh, knee, no,
I saw nothing.
I saw no knee
no luscious thigh
no slither belt,
with lace embroidered border
that was hardly a border at all.

I was looking for the worm in my glass.

I thought about her after,
when I was high above St Louis.
I'm glad I didn't see
her silk white thighs
her red satin suspender belt

with black embroidered border
that was hardly a border at all.

I swear to you
I saw nothing,
not even the worm
lying on his back
waiting to penetrate my tongue.

Hannah Binding Shoes

Poor lone Hannah,
Sitting at the window, binding shoes:
Faded, wrinkled,
Sitting, stitching, in a mournful muse.
Bright-eyed beauty once was she,
When the bloom was on the tree:
Spring and winter,
Hannah's at the window, binding shoes.

Not a neighbor,
Passing nod or answer will refuse,
To her whisper,
'Is there from the fishers any news?'
Oh, her heart's adrift, with one
On an endless voyage gone!
Night and morning,
Hannah's at the window, binding shoes.

Fair young Hannah,
Ben, the sunburnt fisher, gayly woos:
Hale and clever,
For a willing heart and hand he sues.
May-day skies are all aglow,
And the waves are laughing so!
For her wedding
Hannah leaves her window and her shoes.

May is passing:
'Mid the apple boughs a pigeon cooes.

Hannah shudders,
For the mild southwester mischief brews.
  Round the rocks of Marblehead,
  Outward bound, a schooner sped:
    Silent, lonesome
Hannah's at the window, binding shoes.

    'Tis November,
Now no tear her wasted cheek bedews.
    From Newfoundland
Not a sail returning will she lose,
  Whispering hoarsely, 'Fishermen,
  Have you, have you heard of Ben?'
    Old with watching,
Hannah's at the window, binding shoes.

    Twenty winters
Bleach and tear the ragged shore she views.
    Twenty seasons –
Never one has brought her any news.
  Still her dim eyes silently
  Chase the white sails o'er the sea:
    Hopeless, faithful,
Hannah's at the window, binding shoes.

ALICE KAVOUNAS

The Man in The Lacoste Shirt

America has pinked your cheeks.
The lines that hem your eyes reveal
nothing but laughter.
Years of tennis have taught you how to grip
another man's hand without flinching.
And you're a prime example of the lean
expensive cuts
that don't marble the flesh.

It's taken you nearly fifty years
of crossing borders
to reach this bed
to annex this dark-haired
olive-skinned
slash American,
living in another country.

You could drown in your own innocence.
The alligators basking in your bedroom closet
will emerge each night
to clasp you with their scaly tails
while you stand naked
in a pool of Connecticut moonlight.

C. P. CAVAFY

Chosen by Alice Kavounas

Picture of a Youth Twenty-three Years Old

Painted by his friend of the same age, an amateur

He finished the picture
Yesterday at midday. Now
Looks at it in detail.
He has painted him in
A grey unbuttoned coat,
A dark grey; and without
A waistcoat or a tie;
And in a rosepink shirt;
And open at the throat,
So something may be seen
Of its beauty, a sight
Of breast and neck breathing.
His forehead on the right
All of it is nearly
Covered by his hair,
His beautiful and bright
Hair (as he thinks the right
Way to part it this year).
There is the expression
Completely sensuous
He wanted to put in
When he was doing the eyes,
When he was doing the lips . . .
His mouth, his lips which are
For the fulfilment of
Exquisite lovemaking.

A White African Dress

Yesterday, as I thought about what my father wore
That Sunday in Abuja when we first met,
A huge heron lit up my path through the woods
Far from the river bank where the bird
Usually stood, grave as a prayer.

It flew ahead of me away from the water –
Its huge wings hesitating like a heavy heart –
Through gold leaves fluttering from the bright trees.
He was dressed all in white, my father;
A long white African dress, ornate like lace,

Repeating its pattern in intricate stitching.
The bright white lit up his black face.
My father chanted and ranted and prayed at my feet
creating wings with his hands, *Oh God Almighty*,
My hands, clasped tightly, nursed on my lap.

He clutched a bible and waved it about
As he sang and danced around the hotel room
Until the Holy book opened its paper aeroplane wings
And my father flew off, his white dress trailing
Like smoke in the sky, all the lovely stitches, dropping

Dropping like silver threads on the dark red land.

MARION ANGUS

Chosen by Jackie Kay

The Blue Jacket

When there comes a flower to the stingles nettle,
To the hazel bushes, bees,
I think I can see my little sister
Rocking herself by the hazel trees.

Rocking her arms for very pleasure
That every leaf so sweet can smell,
And that she has on the warm blue jacket
Of mine, she liked so well.

Oh to win near you, little sister!
To hear your soft lips say —
'I'll never tak' up wi' lads or lovers,
But a baby I maun hae.

'A baby in a cradle rocking,
Like a nut, in a hazel shell,
And a new blue jacket, like this o' Annie's,
It sets me aye sae well.'

CHRISTOPHER LOGUE

Hector Appears on the Battlefield

Go close.

Besides his helmet and his loincloth Hector wore
A battle-skirt of silver mesh,
Its band, a needlepoint procession:
Sangárian tigers, each with a lifted paw.

The Gate swings down.

On either forearm as on either shin
Lightweight self-sprung wraparound guards
Decked with a slash of yellow chrome without
Dotted with silver knots and stars within.
And now –
As he moves through the light
Downwards along the counterslope, his shield,
Whose rim's ceramic fold will shatter bronze
Whose 16 alternating gold and silver radiants
Burst from an adamant medusa-Aphrodité boss
(Its hair bouffant with venomous eels
The pupils of its bullet-starred-glass eyes
Catching the sun) catching the sun
Chylábborak, Aeneas and Anáxapart,
Quibuph, Kykéon, Akafáct and Palt
Cantering their chariots to the right of his,
His silver mittens up (a perfect fit,
They go with everything)
Sarpédon, Gray, Bárbarinth, Hágnet, Ábassee,

His favourite brother,
Cantering their chariots to his left:

    'Still . . .'

ALEXANDER POPE

Chosen by Christopher Logue

Belinda Gets Dressed
from The Rape of The Lock

With varying vanities, from ev'ry part,
They shift the moving toy-shop of their heart;
Where wigs with wigs, with sword-knots sword-knots strive,
Beaux banish beaux, and coaches coaches drive.
This erring mortals levity may call,
Oh, blind to truth! the sylphs contrive it all.
   'Of these am I, who thy protection claim,
A watchful sprite, and Ariel is my name.
Late, as I ranged the crystal wilds of air,
In the clear mirror of thy ruling star
I saw, alas! some dread event impend,
Ere to the main this morning sun descend;
But heaven reveals not what, or how, or where:
Warn'd by the sylph, oh, pious maid, beware!
This to disclose is all thy guardian can:
Beware of all, but most beware of man!'
   He said; when Shock, who thought she slept too long,
Leap'd up, and waked his mistress with his tongue.
'Twas then, Belinda, if report say true,
Thy eyes first open'd on a billet-doux;
Wounds, charms, and ardours, were no sooner read,
But all the vision vanish'd from thy head.
   And now, unveil'd, the toilet stands display'd,
Each silver vase in mystic order laid.
First, robed in white, the nymph intent adores,
With head uncover'd, the cosmetic powers.
A heav'nly image in the glass appears,
To that she bends, to that her eye she rears;

Th' inferior priestess, at her altar's side,
Trembling, begins the sacred rites of pride.
Unnumber'd treasures ope at once, and here
The various offerings of the world appear;
From each she nicely culls with curious toil,
And decks the goddess with the glitt'ring spoil.
This casket India's glowing gems unlocks,
And all Arabia breathes from yonder box.
The tortoise here and elephant unite,
Transform'd to combs, the speckled and the white.
Here files of pins extend their shining rows,
Puffs, powders, patches, Bibles, billet-doux.
Now awful beauty puts on all its arms;
The fair each moment rises in her charms,
Repairs her smiles, awakens every grace,
And calls forth all the wonders of her face:
Sees by degrees a purer blush arise,
And keener lightnings quicken in her eyes.
The busy sylphs surround their darling care,
These set the head, and those divide the hair,
Some fold the sleeve, while others plait the gown;
And Betty's praised for labours not her own.

CAROLA LUTHER

Nineteen Thirties Suit

Hassock and tussock, and lake by night, my lining
sliding around the inside white of your arm.
Hidden in the smell of man there is the farm,
the obstinate animals (let go, let go and settle
down, their steam, the hay is warm, is kind,
their dreams a nudge, a pushing down
the blissful mud, the sup). Get up.

Tonight we're clean, my crease pressed
hard along your length of thigh, keen
with intention like mind, like money, comfortable
you, high on your legs, your fine leather shoes,
my tweed holding and falling in folds,
in pleats, in darts from waist, from hips,
smoothed over arse, and the swinging skirt

of a jacket lifted, pocket, waistband, steady,
worsted, gathering together the cocky white starch
of your shirt. We arrive at the door. I softly turn
your thoughts to peppers, orange and green,
remind your blind tongue of its search for pips in the pear,
draw your attention to cups, the drop of tulips
half-closed and demure in a turquoise vase.

You appraise the poise of a woman full to the brim
in her skin, the wide cascade of that frock,
the way it sways its dark-red bell (she is the belle
of this party), introduce the idea of light

you might find in a fuchsia tent, imagine going down,
going under, the bowl of skirt outside like a gentle house,
while beneath, in here, the secret life of thighs.

SAPPHO

Chosen by Carola Luther

'I hear that Andromeda'

I hear that Andromeda –

That hayseed in her hay-
seed finery – has put
a torch to your heart

and she without even
the art of lifting her
skirt over her ankles

Translated from the Greek by Mary Barnard

ROGER McGOUGH

Your Favourite Hat

Believe me when I tell you that
I long to be your favourite hat

The velvet one. Purply-black
With ribbons trailing at the back

The one you wear to parties, plays,
Assignations on red-letter days

Like a bat in your unlit hall
I'd hang until there came the call

To freedom. To hug your crown
As you set off through Camden Town

To run my fingers through your hair
Unbeknown in Chalcot Square

To let them linger, let them trace
My shadow cast upon your face

Until, on reaching the appointed place
(The pulse at your temple, feel it race!)

Breathless, you whisper: 'At last, at last.'
And once inside, aside I'm cast

There to remain as time ticks by
Nap rising at each moan and sigh

Ecstatic, curling at the brim
To watch you naked, there with him

Until, too soon, the afternoon gone
You retrieve me, push me on

Then take your leave (as ever, in haste)
Me eager to devour the taste

Of your hair. Your temples now on fire
My tongue, the hatband as you perspire

To savour the dampness of your skin
As you window-gaze. Looking in

But not seeing. Over Primrose Hill
You dawdle, relaxed now, until

Home Sweet Home, where, safely back
Sighing, you impale me on the rack

Is it in spite or because of that
I long to be your favourite hat?

A. S. J. TESSIMOND

Chosen by Roger McGough

The Man in the Bowler Hat

I am the unnoticed, the unnoticeable man:
The man who sat on your right in the morning train:
The man you looked through like a windowpane:
The man who was the colour of the carriage, the colour of the
    mounting
Morning pipe smoke.

I am the man too busy with a living to live,
Too hurried and worried to see and smell and touch:
The man who is patient too long and obeys too much
And wishes too softly and seldom.

I am the man they call the nation's backbone,
Who am boneless – playable catgut, pliable clay:
The Man they label Little lest one day
I dare to grow.

I am the rails on which the moment passes,
The megaphone for many words and voices:
I am graph, diagram,
Composite face.

I am the led, the easily-fed,
The tool, the not-quite-fool,
The would-be-safe-and-sound.
The uncomplaining bound,
The dust fine-ground,
Stone-for-a-statue waveworn pebble-round.

IAN McMILLAN

Big Pants on the Washing Line in the Wind

Like
Distant mountains, shaking in an earthquake.
Flags of surrender.
Faces of kids queuing for ice cream.

Like
Tents on a high cliff in a howling storm.
Butterflies you wouldn't want to meet.
The kind of fruit you'd love to carry home.

Big pants
Big pants
Let the gale carry you
And make you dance!

PAN CHIEH-YU

Chosen by Ian McMillan

Resentful Song

White silk of *Ch'I*, newly torn out,
Spotlessly pure as the frozen snow,
Cut to make a fan of conjoined happiness,
Round as the moon at its brightest.
It is ever in and out of my master's sleeve
And its movement makes a gentle breeze.
But oft I fear with the Autumn's coming
When cold blasts drive away the torrid heat
It will be cast aside into a chest
And love, in mid-course, will end.

SARAH MAGUIRE

The Invisible Mender
(My First Mother)

I'm sewing on new buttons
to this washed silk shirt.
Mother of pearl,
I chose them carefully.
In the haberdashers on Chepstow Place
I turned a boxful over
one by one,
searching for the backs with flaws:
those blemished green or pink or aubergine,
small birth marks on the creamy shell.

These afternoons are short,
the sunlight buried after three or four,
sap in the cold earth.
The trees are bare.
I'm six days late.
My right breast aches so
when I bend to catch a fallen button
that strays across the floor.
Either way,
there'll be blood on my hands.

Thirty-seven years ago you sat in poor light
and sewed your time away,
then left.
But I'm no good at this:
a peony of blood gathers on my thumb, falls
then widens on the shirt like a tiny, opening mouth.

I think of you like this –
as darkness comes,
as the window that I can't see through
is veiled with mist
which turns to condensation
slipping down tall panes of glass,
a mirror to the rain outside –
and I know that I'll not know
if you still are mending in the failing light,
or if your hands (as small as mine)
lie still now, clasped together, underground.

JOHN DONNE

Chosen by Sarah Maguire

The Funerall

Who ever comes to shroud me, do not harme
 Nor question much
That subtle wreath of haire, which crowns my arme;
The mystery, the signe you must not touch,
 For 'tis my outward Soule,
Viceroy to that, which unto heaven being gone,
 Will leave this to controule,
And keep these limbes, her Provinces, from dissolution.

For if the sinewie thread my braine lets fall
 Through every part,
Can tye those parts, and make mee one of all;
These haires which upward grew, and strength and art
 Have from a better braine,
Can better do'it; Except she meant that I
 By this should know my pain,
As prisoners then are manacled, when they'are condemn'd to die.

What ere shee meant by'it, bury it with me,
 For since I am
Loves martyr, it might breed idolatrie,
If into others hands these Reliques came;
 As'twas humility
To afford to it all that a Soule can doe,
 So,'tis some bravery,
That since you would save none of mee, I bury some of you.

Valentine

My sister phones to tell me that she found
when stripping old wallpaper from the hall
in thick black marker writ my name –
paula meehan kiss kiss love love – then yours,

enclosed within a heart. An arrow. The ground
shifts. I'd forgotten all that. I can call
to mind my nineteenth year with ease – the hames
we made of the job, woodchip (rough as furze

on the hands) overpainted green, the sound
of Dylan in mono, the rise and the fall
of your breath as you came and you went and you came,
as you did and you didn't, first mine, then hers,

then mine again. Never again. I'd sooner eat my
words, the wall they're written on. I'd sooner die.

Chosen by Paula Meehan

A Gulling Sonnet

The sacred muse that first made love divine
   Hath made him naked and without attire;
But I will clothe him with this pen of mine
   That all the world his fashion will admire:
His hat of hope, his band of beauty fine,
   His cloak of craft, his doublet of desire;
Grief for a girdle shall about him twine,
   His points of pride, his eyelet-holes of ire,
His hose of hate, his codpiece of conceit,
   His stockings of stern strife, his shirt of shame;
His garters of vain-glory, gay and slight,
   His pantofles of passion will I frame;
     Pumps of presumption shall adorn his feet,
     And socks of sullenness exceeding sweet.

ADRIAN MITCHELL

Jake's Amazing Suit

When you see me in my suit –
You'll look and at first
All you'll see is a burst
Of shimmering electric blue.
Then you'll focus in and see
That the vision is me
And I'm walking
And my suit is walking too

When you see me in my suit –
Flowing soft as milk
It'll be Thailand silk
That follows any move at all.
And its cut and its drape
Will lay on me a shape
Like I'm standing
Underneath a waterfall.

When you see me in my suit –
    I won't be able to walk out in public
    Because of my wonderful threads
    Never mind, instead
    We'll spend our life in bed
    With nothing but love in our heads
When you see me in my suit

I once saw Miles Davis
Walk across the tarmac to an aeroplane.

Yes I once saw Miles Davis walking
Oh now let me explain –

His face was carved from a living mahogany tree-trunk.
He wore power sunglasses over his eyes
With silver pistons connected to his ears.
His beret sat on the top of his head
Like a little powder-blue cloud
And when he smiled – it turned you to stone.

His suit was four-and-a-half times too big for his body.
It was kind of a tweed woven out of mountain light.
It had criss-cross lines of the sort of luminous
Green you only see on the top of birthday cakes.

I once saw Miles Davis
Walk across the tarmac from an aeroplane
Yes I once saw Miles Davis
I can explain –

I want a suit like that
I want a suit like that
I want a suit so electric
If I leave it alone
It'll jump off its hanger
Take a walk on its own
Give me a suit like that
Give me a suit like that

So that my love will love me
Even more than she loves me now
When she sees me in my suit.

ROBERT HERRICK

Chosen by Adrian Mitchell

Upon Julia's Clothes

Whenas in silks my Julia goes,
Then, then, methinks, how sweetly flows
The liquefaction of her clothes.

Next, when I cast mine eyes and see
That brave vibration each way free;
O how that glittering taketh me!

Cast Out

She wears a black cowl round her head, her grey hem sweeps
    the dust.
She circles my walled city with her clappers and her cup.

From battlement and organ-loft I throw her food to eat:
unleavened bread, goat's cheese, the flesh of swine. But God
    forbid

she draw the water from my well or raise her lips to mine.
I fill my mouth with cloves. I hold my nose. I breathe into

a handkerchief of lace. All night I hear her pace.
I douse myself with vinegar, rose-water, eau-de-vie.

She calls my name. She rattles at the locks. She drinks the
    slurry
from the trough. She shadows me in dreams. I pray to God,

'Oh let it end. Enough!' She's shed her eyebrows, lost her
    sense
of touch. Her voice is like the toad's. The priests call out

'Leviticus, Leviticus'; perform her funeral rite,
as it behoves, beside the fresh-dug pit. The coffin waits;

the winding-sheet, the spices and the spade; the carrion crow.
I sprinkle her with clay, ignore her cries. I turn away

to ring the Requiem bell. She joins the living dead.
At Mass I see her lean into the leper-squint, receive

from some gloved hand the Sacred Host. Until Christ comes to
   rest
upon my tongue, I live in dread. My palace is a Spittle House.

I wear beneath my robe her running sores. Under my hood,
her face.

Donal Og

It is late last night the dog was speaking of you;
the snipe was speaking of you in her deep marsh.
It is you are the lonely bird through the woods;
and that you may be without a mate until you find me.

You promised me, and you said a lie to me,
that you would be before me where the sheep are flocked;
I gave a whistle and three hundred cries to you,
and I found nothing there but a bleating lamb.

You promised me a thing that was hard for you,
a ship of gold under a silver mast;
twelve towns with a market in all of them,
and a fine white court by the side of the sea.

You promised me a thing that is not possible,
that you would give me gloves of the skin of a fish;
that you would give me shoes of the skin of a bird;
and a suit of the dearest silk in Ireland.

When I go by myself to the Well of Loneliness,
I sit down and I go through my trouble;
when I see the world and do not see my boy,
he that has an amber shade in his hair.

It was on that Sunday I gave my love to you;
the Sunday that is last before Easter Sunday.
And myself on my knees reading the Passion;
and my two eyes giving love to you for ever.

My mother said to me not to be talking with you today,
or tomorrow, or on the Sunday;
it was a bad time she took for telling me that;
it was shutting the door after the house was robbed.

My heart is as black as the blackness of the sloe,
or as the black coal that is on the smith's forge;
or as the sole of a shoe left in white halls;
it was you put that darkness over my life.

You have taken the east from me; you have taken the west
from me;
you have taken what is before me and what is behind me;
you have taken the moon, you have taken the sun from me;
and my fear is great that you have taken God from me!

Translated from the Irish by Lady Augusta Gregory

Red Gloves

Reaching the restaurant late
I find the empty shells
of your gloves on the cold curb:

stretchy, crushed red velvet
which slithered off your lap
to float in the sodium stream.

What could they mean except
you have arrived before me
and taken your place already?

The things we forget or lose
live in a heaven of debris
waiting for us to collect them;

already your naked hands
are fluttering over the table
missing they don't know what.

THOMAS HARDY

Chosen by Andrew Motion

She at His Funeral

They bear him to his resting-place —
In slow procession sweeping by;
I follow at a stranger's space;
His kindred they, his sweetheart I.
Unchanged my gown of garish dye,
Though sable-sad is their attire;
But they stand round with griefless eye,
Whilst my regret consumes like fire!

PAUL MULDOON

The Treaty

My grandfather. Frank Regan, cross-shanked, his shoulders in
    a moult,
steadies the buff
of his underparts against the ledge of the chimney-bluff
of the mud-walled house in Cullenramer

in which, earlier, he had broken open a bolt
of the sky-stuff
and held it to the failing light, having himself failed to balance
    Gormley's cuffs.
'This Collins,' Gormley had wagged, 'is a right flimflammer.'

Cross-shanked against the chimney-bluff, he's sizing up what
    follows
from our being on the verge
of nation-

hood when another broad-lapelled, swallow-tailed swallow
comes at a clip through the dusk-blue serge
to make some last minute alterations.

Chosen by Paul Muldoon

Man in the Long Black Coat

Crickets are chirpin', the water is high,
There's a soft cotton dress on the line hangin' dry,
Window wide open, African trees
Bent over backwards from a hurricane breeze.
Not a word of goodbye, not even a note,
She gone with the man
In the long black coat.

Somebody seen him hanging around
At the old dance hall on the outskirts of town.
He looked into her eyes when she stopped him to ask
If he wanted to dance, he had a face like a mask.
Somebody said from the Bible he'd quote
There was dust on the man
In the long black coat.

Preacher was a talkin', there's a sermon he gave,
He said every man's conscience is vile and depraved,
You cannot depend on it to be your guide
When it's you who must keep it satisfied.
It ain't easy to swallow, it sticks in the throat,
She gave her heart to the man
In the long black coat.

There are no mistakes in life some people say
It is true sometimes you can see it that way.
But people don't live or die, people just float.
She went with the man
In the long black coat.

There's smoke on the water, it's been there since June,
Tree trunks uprooted, 'neath the high crescent moon
Feel the pulse and vibration and the rumbling force
Somebody is out there beating a dead horse.
She never said nothing, there was nothing she wrote,
She gone with the man
In the long black coat.

GRACE NICHOLS

The Fat Black Woman Versus Politics

The fat black woman
could see through politicians
like snake sees through rat
she knows the oil
that ease the tongue
she knows the soup-mouth tact
she knows the game
the lame race for fame
she knows the slippery hammer
wearing down upon the brain

In dreams she's seen them
stalking the corridors of power
faces behind a ballot-box cover
the fat black woman won't be their lover

But if you were to ask her
What's your greatest political ambition?
she'll be sure to answer

    To feed powercrazy politicians a manifesto of lard
    To place my X against a bowl of custard

FEDERICO GARCIA LORCA

Chosen by Grace Nichols

Treeney Treeney

Treeney treeney
dry and greeny.

The girl with the beautiful face
is out picking olives.
The wind, suitor of towers,
holds her tightly round the waist.
Four riders passed by on mares
from Andalusia
in fancy suits of blue and green,
with long dark capes.
'Come to Cordova, young miss.'
The girl doesn't listen.
Three bull fighting boys
passed by, so slim in the waist,
in suits colored orange
with swords of old silver.
'Come to Sevilla, young miss.'
The girl doesn't listen.
When the afternoon fell
purple-dim, the light diffused,
a young man passed who carried
moon myrtle and roses.
'Come to Granada, young miss.'
And the girl doesn't listen.
The girl with the beautiful face
goes on picking olives,

with the wind's gray arm
encircling her waist.

Treeney treeney
dry and greeny.

Translated by Will Kirkland

Cousin Coat

You are my secret coat. You're never dry.
You wear the weight and stink of black canals.
Malodorous companion, we know why
It's taken me so long to see we're pals,
To learn why my acquaintance never sniff
Or send me notes to say I stink of stiff.

But you don't talk, historical bespoke.
You must be worn, be intimate as skin,
And though I never lived what you invoke,
At birth I was already buttoned in.
Your clammy itch became my atmosphere,
An air made half of anger, half of fear.

And what you are is what I tried to shed
In libraries with Donne and Henry James.
You're here to bear a message from the dead
Whose history's dishonoured with their names.
You mean the North, the poor, and troopers sent
To shoot down those who showed their discontent.

No comfort there for comfy meliorists
Grown weepy over Jarrow photographs.
No comfort when the poor the state enlists
Parade before their fathers' cenotaphs.
No comfort when the strikers all go back
To see which twenty thousand get the sack.

Be with me when they cauterise the facts.
Be with me to the bottom of the page,

Insisting on what history exacts.
Be memory, be conscience, will and rage,
And keep me cold and honest, cousin coat,
So if I lie, I'll know you're at my throat.

HOMER

Chosen by Sean O'Brien

Vulcan Forges the Armour of Achilles
from The Iliad

Then first he form'd th' immense and solid *Shield*;
Rich, various Artifice emblaz'd the Field;
Its utmost Verge a threefold Circle bound;
A silver Chain suspends the massy Round,
Five ample Plates the broad Expanse compose,
And god-like Labours on the Surface rose.
There shone the Image of the Master Mind:
There Earth, there Heav'n, there Ocean he design'd;
Th' unweary'd Sun, the Moon compleatly round;
The starry Lights that Heav'ns high Convex crown'd;
The *Pleiads, Hyads*, with the Northern Team;
And great *Orion's* more refulgent Beam;
To which, around the Axle of the Sky,
The *Bear* revolving, points his golden Eye,
Still shines exalted on th' ætherial Plain,
Nor bathes his blazing Forehead in the Main.
Two Cities radiant on the Shield appear,
The Image one of Peace, and one of War.
Here sacred Pomp, and genial Feast delight
And solemn Dance, and *Hymenœal* Rite;
Along the Street the new-made Brides are led,
With Torches flaming, to the nuptial Bed;
The youthful Dancers in a Circle bound
To the soft Flute, and Cittern's silver Sound:
Thro' the fair Streets, the Matrons in a Row,
Stand in their Porches, and enjoy the Show.
There, in the *Forum* swarm a num'rous Train;
The Subject of Debate, a Townsman slain:

One pleads the Fine discharg'd, which one deny'd,
And bade the Publick and the Laws decide:
The Witness is produc'd on either Hand;
For this, or that, the partial People stand:
Th' appointed Heralds still the noisy Bands,
And form a Ring, with Scepters in their Hands;
On Seats of Stone, within the sacred Place,
The rev'rend Elders nodded o'er the Case;
Alternate, each th' attesting Scepter took,
And rising solemn, each his Sentence spoke.
Two golden Talents lay amidst, in sight,
The Prize of him who best adjudg'd the Right.
Another Part (a Prospect diff'ring far)
Glow'd with refulgent Arms, and horrid War.
Two mighty Hosts a leaguer'd Town embrace,
And one would pillage, one wou'd burn the Place.
Meantime the Townsmen, arm'd with silent Care,
A secret Ambush on the Foe prepare:
Their Wives, their Children, and the watchful Band
Of trembling Parents on the Turrets stand.
They march; by *Pallas* and by *Mars* made bold;
Gold were the Gods, their radiant Garments Gold,
And Gold their Armour: These the Squadron led,
August, Divine, Superior by the Head!
A Place for Ambush fit, they found, and stood
Cover'd with Shields, beside a silver Flood.
Two Spies at distance lurk, and watchful seem
If Sheep or Oxen seek the winding Stream.
Soon the white Flocks proceeded o'er the Plains,
And Steers slow-moving, and two Shepherd Swains;
Behind them, piping on their Reeds, they go,
Nor fear an Ambush, nor suspect a Foe.
In Arms the glitt'ring Squadron rising round

Rush sudden; Hills of Slaughter heap the Ground,
Whole Flocks and Herds lye bleeding on the Plains,
And, all amidst them, dead, the Shepherd Swains!
The bellowing Oxen the Besiegers hear;
They rise, take Horse, approach, and meet the War;
They fight, they fall, beside the silver Flood;
The waving Silver seem'd to blush with Blood.
There Tumult, there Contention stood confest;
One rear'd a Dagger at a Captive's Breast,
One held a living Foe, that freshly bled
With new-made Wounds; another dragg'd a dead;
Now here, now there, the Carcasses they tore:
Fate stalk'd amidst them, grim with human Gore.
And the whole War came out, and met the Eye;
And each bold Figure seem'd to live, or die.

Translated by Alexander Pope

Well-Heeled

So what's to live for?
I'm placing a Gold American Express card
on the cash desk – seven hundred and fifty dollars
down the drain
for a fantasy rhinestone pump
with spike heels.
Yesterday, it was paisley-gilded
black brocade lace-ups with a louis heel.
My analyst said, 'Indulge.'
So I'm indulging already!
I think I'd rather have an affair.
My grecian slave sandals
would come in handy for that
or maybe my fuchsia satin court shoes –
depending on the man.

I started my girls off right.
As soon as they put a foot on terra firma
I got them little Edwardian slippers:
pink sides with a white toe and bow.
I can still see them teetering along
with frilly cotton socks and Easter bonnets.
I have those shoes up in the attic someplace.
I wonder which box they're in . . .

Nobody gives a damn about shoes anymore.
Will Sammy the Hong Kong mailman
want to seduce me in my red-rabbit-fur bedroom slippers?
Who's to appreciate – Glen, my spouse?

What a joke!
He trots off in his Gucci loafers to work
and you might as well be wearing
hiking boots under your negligee
for all he cares.
So I head for Neiman-Marcus Shoe Salon –
'the place for women who love shoes'.
If he doesn't notice my fantasy pumps
maybe he'll notice the bill next month
from American Express.
I had a pair of Maud Frizon shoes
that had cute fake watches on the ankle straps.
He kept mocking them by kneeling down in front of me
'to see what time it is'.

*Did you tell that shrink of yours
about the Calvin Klein princess pumps
ya bought a year ago
and have never worn cause you say
they're too pretty to wear
or your Texan snake and pony skin
hand-tooled leather cowboy boots
that you wear to the supermarket –
did ya tell him that –
what does all this mean?*
Glen always toys with the dramatic
rather than the mundane in our relationship.

It was a pair of white patent Mary Janes
that made me the way I am today.
I refused to unfasten the strap
out of its golden buckle.
I wore them to bed, to school,
to play in – I even took a bath

with them on once – they made me happy.
One morning I woke up
and they were gone.
Words cannot convey that catastrophe.

Last week I wore a sea-green
suede-fronded ankle-boot
on my head to a party.
I went barefoot.
Maybe this is a development.

from The Midnight Court

If I was as slow as some I know
To stand up for my rights and my dress a show,
Some brainless, illbred, country mope
You could understand if I lost hope;
But ask the first you meet by chance:
Hurling match or race or dance,
Pattern or party, market or fair,
Whatever it was, was I not there?
And didn't I make a good impression
Turning up in the height of fashion?
· My hair was washed and combed and powdered,
My coif like snow and stiffly laundered;
I'd a little white hood with ribbons and ruff
On a spotted dress of the finest stuff,
And facings to show off the line
Of a cardinal cloak the colour of wine;
A cambric apron filled with showers
Of fruit and birds and trees and flowers;
Neatly-fitting, expensive shoes
With the highest of heels pegged up with screws;
Silken gloves, and myself in spangles
Of brooches, buckles, rings and bangles.
And you mustn't imagine I was shy,
The sort that slinks with a downcast eye,
Solitary, lonesome, cold and wild,
Like a mountainy girl or an only child.
I tossed my cap at the crowds of the races
And kept my head in the toughest places.

Am I not always on the watch
At bonfire, dance or hurling match,
Or outside the chapel after Mass
To coax a smile from fellows that pass?
But I'm wasting my time on a wildgoose-chase,
And my spirit's broken – and that's my case!
After all my shaping, sulks and passions
All my aping of styles and fashions,
All the times that my cards were spread
And my hands were read and my cup was read;
Every old rhyme, pishrogue and rune,
Crescent, full moon and harvest moon,
Whit and All Souls and the First of May,
I've nothing to show for all they say.

Translated from the Irish by Frank O'Connor

DENNIS O'DRISCOLL

Success Story

Your name is made.
You have turned the company around,
downsized franchise operations,
increased market penetration
on the leisure side,
returned the focus to core business.
Man of the Month in the export journal,
ruffler of feathers, raiser of dust,
at the height of your abilities.

You don't suspect it yet, but things
are destined to go gradually downhill.
This year or the next you will
barely notice any change – your tan offsets
the thinning of your blow-dried hair,
you recharge your batteries
with longer weekend snooze-ins,
treat back trouble with heat pad and massage,
install an ergonomic chair for daytime comfort.

Behind closed boardroom doors
there will be talk: not quite
the man you were, losing your grip,
ideas a bit blah, in danger
of becoming a spent force.
The prospect of an early
severance package will be tested
delicately over coffee, low-key as
'Can you pass the sugar, please?'

The flamboyant young blood you trained
will start talking down, interrupting
half-way through your report
on grasping brassplate opportunities.
You will hear yourself say *In my day*
more often than you should.
Bite your tongue.
Brighten your tie.
Show your old readiness to fight.

MARINA TSVETAEVA

Chosen by Dennis O'Driscoll

We Shall Not Escape Hell

We shall not escape Hell, my passionate
sisters, we shall drink black resins –
we who sang our praises to the Lord
with every one of our sinews, even the finest,

we did not lean over cradles or
spinning wheels at night, and now we are
carried off by an unsteady boat
under the skirts of a sleeveless cloak,

we dressed every morning in
fine Chinese silk, and we would
sing our paradisal songs at
the fire of the robbers' camp,

slovenly needlewomen, (all
our sewing came apart), dancers,
players upon pipes: we have been
the queens of the whole world!

first scarcely covered by rags,
then with constellations in our hair, in
gaol and at feasts we have
bartered away heaven,

in starry nights, in the apple
orchards of Paradise.
– Gentle girls, my beloved sisters,
we shall certainly find ourselves in Hell!

Translated from the Russian by Elaine Feinstein

ALICE OSWALD

Wedding

From time to time our love is like a sail
and when the sail begins to alternate
from tack to tack, it's like a swallowtail
and when the swallow flies it's like a coat;
and if the coat is yours, it has a tear
like a wide mouth and when the mouth begins
to draw the wind, it's like a trumpeter
and when the trumpet blows, it blows like millions
and this, my love, when millions come and go
beyond the need of us, is like a trick;
and when the trick begins, it's like a toe
tip-toeing on a rope, which is like luck;
and when the luck begins, it's like a wedding,
which is like love, which is like everything.

DAVID SHAW

Chosen by Alice Oswald

The Wark o' the Weavers

We're all met together here to sit and to crack
With our glasses in our hands and our wark upon our back
For there isna a tradesman that can either mend or mak'
But what wears the wark o' the weavers.

If it werena the weavers what would we do?
We wouldna hae claith made of our woo'
We wouldna hae a coat, neither black nor blue,
If it werena for the wark o' the weavers.

There's folk independent of other tradesmen's wark,
For women need no barber and dykers need no clerk,
But none of them can do without a coat or a sark,
Which must be the wark o' some weaver.

The ploughmen lads they mock us and crack aye about's,
And say we are thin-faced, bleached-like clouts,
But yet for all their mockery they canna do without's,
No they canna want the wark o' the weavers.

There's smiths and there's wrights and there's masons and a',
There's doctors and dominies and men that live by law,
And our friends in South America, though them we never
    saw,
And they all need the wark o' the weavers.

Our soldiers and our sailors, o'd, we make them all bold,
For gin they hadna claes, faith, they couldna fecht for cold,
The high and low, the rich and poor, a'body, young and old,
They all need the wark o' the weavers.

So the weaving's a trade that never can fail,
While we aye need a clout to hold another hale,
So let us now be merry ower a beaker of good ale,
And drink to the health of the weavers.

The Appointment

Flamingo silk. New ruff,
the ivory ghost
of a halter. Chestnut curls,

commas behind the ear.
'Taller, by half a head,
than my lord Walsingham.'

His Devon-cream brogue,
malt eyes. New cloak
mussed in her mud.

The Queen leans forward,
a rosy envelope of civet:
a cleavage

whispering seed-pearls.
Her own sleeve
rubs that speck of dirt

on his cheek. Three thousand
ornamental fruit baskets
swing in the smoke.

'It is our pleasure
to have our servant trained
some longer time

in Ireland.' Stamp out
marks of the Irish.
Their saffron smocks.

All carroughs, bards
and rhymers. Desmonds
and Fitzgeralds

stuck on low spikes,
an avenue of heads
to the war-tent.

Kerry timber
sold to the Canaries.
Pregnant girls

hung in their own hair
on city walls. Plague
crumpling gargoyles

through Munster. 'They spoke
like ghosts crying
out of their graves.'

Disillusionment of Ten O'Clock

The houses are haunted
By white night-gowns.
None are green.
Or purple with green rings,
Or green with yellow rings,
Or yellow with blue rings.
None of them are strange,
With socks of lace
And beaded ceintures.
People are not going
To dream of baboons and periwinkles.
Only, here and there, an old sailor,
Drunk and asleep in his boots,
Catches tigers
In red weather.

CRAIG RAINE

Mother Dressmaking

The budgerigar pecks at the millet,
his beak prised apart like a pistachio nut

by the fat kernel of tongue. I draw,
wet profiles on the window pane.

We are immersed in making things.
The clock clicks its tongue . . .

trial and error. She tries her shapes
in different ways like a collage,

until they are close without touching . . .
Pinned in place, they are packed

like a suitcase. She takes
a prehistoric triangle of chalk

and leaves a margin for the seams.
Her scissors move through the material

like a swimmer doing crawl,
among the archipelago of tissue paper.

We are immersed, with our tongues out.
Waiting for the time when profiles run.

SIR THOMAS WYATT

Chosen by Craig Raine

'They flee from me that sometime did me seek'

They flee from me that sometime did me seek
With naked foot stalking in my chamber.
I have seen them gentle, tame, and meek
That now are wild and do not remember
That sometime they put themself in danger
To take bread at my hand; and now they range
Busily seeking with a continual change.

Thanked be fortune it hath been otherwise
Twenty times better, but once in special,
In thin array after a pleasant guise,
When her loose gown from her shoulders did fall
And she me caught in her arms long and small,
Therewithal sweetly did me kiss
And softly said, 'Dear heart, how like you this?'

It was no dream: I lay broad waking.
But all is turned thorough my gentleness
Into a strange fashion of forsaking.
And I have leave to go of her goodness
And she also to use newfangleness.
But since that I so kindly am served
I would fain know what she hath deserved.

CAROL RUMENS

The Scarf Exchange

We were playing at adultery when we swapped them
And smuggled them into our marriages.
They were the candid opposite of our bodies,
Our other clothes. They had no wrong-side-out.
Any bit of the fabric could have entered
That almond-size hollow behind our ear-lobes,
Or buttercup-kissed a chin or crept beneath
The hair to snuggle with a feathered nape.
They were perfect hands for sex, never tired or heavy,
Never ashamed. Their only wash was rain.

We left them in public places to betray us.
But no one noticed, heard a single whisper.
They were the softest, most discardable knots
In the wedded world. We gave them everything
– Our pheromones, our microbes, particles
Of street and work and skin, our spit and matter,
All the souls of our days, each soul an odour –
Yet nothing. They were nothing,
A mood, a smoker's sigh. They drifted through us,
Wishing we'd free them from our weight and tangle,
Un-noose them, let them fly. And so, with denser
Threads and knots of air they were re-woven

Until the time when we could cease pretending:
The smell of your life faded, there was only
An image, then, of chequered ash and sky
Too long kept to be returnable.

D. H. LAWRENCE

Chosen by Carol Rumens

In Trouble and Shame

I look at the swaling sunset
And wish I could go also
Through the red doors beyond the black-purple bar.

I wish that I could go
Through the red doors where I could put off
My shame like shoes in the porch,
My pain like garments,
And leave my flesh discarded lying
Like luggage of some departed traveller
Gone one knows not where.

Then I would turn round,
And seeing my cast-off body like lumber,
I would laugh with joy.

Brünhilde

Brünhilde is not a young
woman. She is as old as
God and much heavier. I
am vanquished by her purple
quilted slippers, the way a
whiff of boiled kidney slips from
both the insoles when she walks.
I want to drink out of them,
a good strong rioja with
its own tang set off by hers.
She doesn't insert curlers
but I intend to make her.
They must all be dusty pink:
many of the little prongs
must be worn away or snipped
off leaving small prickly nubs
that catch at my skin when I
nibble her ear. O but her
perfume must be old piss and
Pledge, and I will be her dog,
wear her stiff nylon housecoat;
Brünhilde with her penchant
for Silk Cut, the French poems of
Rilke, her instinct for the
most vivid ways to ripen,
the most vivid ways to rot.

EMILY DICKINSON

'I started Early – Took my Dog'

I started Early – Took my Dog –
And visited the Sea –
The Mermaids in the Basement
Came out to look at me –

And Frigates – in the Upper Floor
Extended Hempen Hands –
Presuming Me to be a Mouse –
Aground – upon the Sands –

But no Man moved Me – till the Tide
Went past my simple Shoe –
And past my Apron – and my Belt
And past my Bodice – too –

And made as He would eat me up –
As wholly as A Dew
Upon a Dandelions's Sleeve –
And then – I started – too –

And He – He followed – close behind –
I felt His Silver Heel
Upon my Ankle – Then my Shoes
Would overflow with Pearl –

Until We met the Solid Town –
No One He seemed to know –
And bowing – with a Mighty look –
At me – The Sea withdrew –

Foreign Tastes

Claudine and you pretended a crush
on the boys in Class Seven.
You were David, pucker-mouthed.

You practiced kissing on the bed.
Claudine was thin and bitey
like one of Alan's ferrets

but her mother was an angel-fish;
an eye-lash flash of blue
and sun-tan orange

with the leopard-skin glamour
of a holiday brochure.
Her house was packed with fat, gold furniture,

waist-high tigers
and bingo-prize buddhas.
A warm aquarium gargled in the corner

and Shirley Bassey sang loud enough
to break a law.
This, your tight-permed mother said,

was because she was foreign
and had unusual tastes.
You thought about this after dark,

imagined that
she'd taste of coconut
and stolen rum,

the tight-throat burn of cigarettes,
hot mud, midnight swimming
and somewhere a long way from Burnley.

And after you were kissed goodnight
you'd stroke your rib-striped chest,
think of foreign things.

I'll Wear Me a Cotton Dress

Oh, will you wear red? Oh, will you wear red?
Oh, will you wear red, Milly Biggers?
'I won't wear red,
It's too much lak Missus' head.
I'll wear me a cotton dress,
Dyed wid copperse an' oak bark.'

Oh, will you wear blue? Oh, will you wear blue?
Oh, will you wear blue, Milly Biggers?
'I won't wear blue,
It's too much lak Missus' shoe.
I'll wear me a cotton dress,
Dyed wid copperse an' oak bark.'

You sholy would wear gray? You sholy would wear gray?
You sholy would wear gray, Milly Biggers?
'I sholy will not wear gray
It's too much lak Missus' way.
I'll wear me a cotton dress,
Dyed wid copperse an' oak bark.'

Well, will you wear white? Well, will you wear white?
Well, will you wear white, Milly Biggers?
'I won't wear wear white,
I'd get dirty long 'fore night.
I'll wear me a cotton dress,
Dyed wid copperse an' oak bark.'

Now, will you wear black? Now, will you wear black?
Now, will you wear black, Milly Biggers?

'I mought wear black,
Case it's de color o' my back;
An' it looks lak my cotton dress,
Dyed wid copperse an' oak bark.'

Stitch in Time

And so he left his wife, just 15 years old, in Gujarat
and travelled back

across three seas
to Taveuni, the Garden Island of Fiji

where he bent once more
to the cloth, spilling from the bench onto the floor,

and moved about the dummy's baste
like a musician round his double bass.

Where, by the hurricane lamp's sepia,
he was the cutter, coatmaker and finisher,

checking and checking again, his stab and pad stitch,
the depth of the gorge, the sleeve's angle of pitch –

a bespoke suit for the local chief,
who was offering (he thinks of his wife, his wife)

an acre of ground in return: his own piece of land
for this man of cloth, made by his hand.

And when they told him where it lay; about the 180 degrees,
the invisible meridian that came over the hill, through the
    coconut trees,

the imaginary chalk mark, where here, tomorrow starts,
and here, today is ending, he felt it in his heart:

the pin-stripe of longitude, the balance, the symmetry,
bisecting time and space, he understood it immediately.

And so ten years later, when he returned for his wife
he brought her back to show her the life

he'd built around that line: the corrugated Meridian Store,
the Meridian Cinema, its screen lifting from the floor

to reveal a boxing ring, every Saturday night.
Then later, the Meridian Garage, with his taxis' headlights

shaking into the dark, sweeping across the bay.
Even the sign was his, with its arrows pointing each way

where tourists stood, a foot each side,
to have their photo taken where the future started and the
    present died.

And that's why, four daughters and a son later, when
his joints were as stiff as his oldest scissors, he went to
    London,

and on his first morning there,
walked alone through the morning air

to Greenwich, to see, at last where it all started.
To stand under a blue sky where the swallows darted:

an explorer discovering the source, the still point after the
    strife,
the first stitch in the pattern to which he'd cut his life.

FERNANDO PESSOA

Chosen by Owen Sheers

The Laundress at the Pool

The laundress at the pool
Pounds clothes upon stone truly.
Sings because sings, is grieving
Because sings because living;
Therefore is cheerful too.

If only I could ever
Succeed in doing with verses
What she does to the clothes,
Maybe I might lose
My destinies, their diverseness.

There's a great unity
In – without any thought,
And half singing, maybe –
Pounding clothes really . . .
Who launders me my heart?

Thread

Before my loose button taps to the floor and sinks
in a rug, I find my stolen hotel mending kit.
What would my grandfather think, the one I never knew,
the tailor, who glided out of war up a still grey Thames,
saw the fog lift on the brick-black face of Wapping?

1910: hats and bulky overcoats, a threat of rain,
a reek of yeast, gulls truant overhead.
He running-stitched, hemmed and collared his way
from Shelter to a Shoreditch flat, then Soho,
near Savile Row, and finally a real house up Finchley Road.
Jews were always middle class, just not allowed to be.

I settle under my desk lamp, open the card,
unravel its tangled blue, then suck and find the eye.
His son's son, a middle class boy (he got me there)
who never sat cross-legged on a table or learnt
chalk's code on cloth or trimmed a weightless astrakhan.

His favourite work was furs. He'd unlock the chest
(the key on a neck-chain) and rifle the silent scraps –
fox and ermine, rabbit and bear – then turn a collar
with his black shears, humming, half-listening
to the city surf of whistles, wheels and cries.

I prod and pull my double thread. One bath a week –
did he smell? A grimy neck? An animal breath
of Polish sausage and tea with blackberry jam?
And what's left of him in me, a softskinned man

who doesn't sing or fast or pray, who bears only
the lost Yiddish scrawled on chest and shoulder?

My grandfather tuts. He taps my final inch, too short
for a knot. *Leave that to me, you've better things to do.*
His eyebrows are thicker than I thought, his breath fainter.
His big-nailed fingers, strong as a fiddler's, undo my work,
dive and twist. His needle a dorsal glint in water.
A quick bite: done. Thread to last a lifetime.

JAN KOCHANOWSKI

Chosen by Henry Shukman

from Laments: VII

Pitiful garments, lamentable dresses
    Of my beloved child –
Why do you draw my sad eyes
    To heap grief on grief?
Never will they clothe
    Her tiny limbs, there is no hope:
She lies gripped in an endless, iron, vice-like sleep.
    Her brightly-patterned summer frocks,
Her ribbons, her gold-studded belts,
    Her mother's gifts, all to no end.
Not to such a bed, dear child,
    Were you to be led.
The wardrobe: a vest and shift –
    Isn't what your mother pledged.
Beneath your head I place a clod of earth:
    Alas! you and your dowry in one chest lie wedged.

Translated from the Polish by Adam Czerniawski

JEAN SPRACKLAND

Dreaming of Rubber Gloves

They'd be as supple as fine suede,
lined with silk cool as leaves.
You'd long for your first pair
as you longed for the white dress,
the bells, the limousine. You'd take on
womanhood the day you entered a shop
with polished wooden floors, the scent
of vanilla. Racks of them
in colours you'd tremble for:
mulberry, azure, a subtle black
that had an idea of brown.
Some cut on the bias, others
ruffled at the wrist, one pair
lustrous like the heart of a shell.
The assistant would measure your fingers
as if for rings, take an impression
in something wet and chalky,
and you'd have her fetch down pairs
to try. Oh you'd know when you saw the ones.

If there was money left you'd buy wine
and that evening set out candles
and cook a special supper.
Later, when the mood was right, you'd put them on
to delight him, and as you stood in the steam
he might come up close behind you,
slide his hands under the froth
and part your glamorous fingers with his own.

ELIZABETH MOODY

Chosen by Jean Sprackland

To Fashion

Gay Fashion thou Goddess so pleasing,
    However imperious thy sway;
Like a mistress capricious and teasing,
    Thy slaves tho' they murmur obey.

The simple, the wise, and the witty,
    The learned, the dunce, and the fool,
The crooked, straight, ugly, and pretty,
    Wear the badge of thy whimsical school.

Tho' thy shape be so fickle and changing,
    That a Proteus thou art to the view;
And our taste so for ever deranging,
    We know not which form to pursue.

Yet wave but thy frolicksome banners,
    And hosts of adherents we see;
Arts, morals, religion, and manners,
    Yield implicit obedience to thee.

More despotic than beauty thy power,
    More than virtue thy rule o'er the mind:
Tho' transient thy reign as a flower,
    That scatters its leaves to the wind.

Ah! while folly thou dealest such measure,
    No matter how fleeting thy day!
Be Wisdom, dear goddess, thy pleasure!
    Then lasting as time be thy stay.

ALICIA STUBBERSFIELD

Jane's Pearls

Rochester called her all day
like you would a dog or cat,
up and down corridors, behind
curtains and in the orchard
where only the owls answered.

The second night he put candles in
her room, opened wardrobes, drawers,
found nothing he'd given to her gone.
He picked up a narrow, suede box,
flicked its little gold catch.

Pearls curled round themselves,
a slight bloom like an apricot.
Each bead different from the next,
each pearl a supplication in his hands,
a rosary he could tell to bring her back.

It fitted round his neck,
hidden under his cravat.
The diamond clasp fixed.
Pearls cool against his sallow skin,
the touch of fingertips at his throat.

CHARLOTTE PERKINS GILMAN

Chosen by Alicia Stubbersfield

This Is a Lady's Hat

This is a lady's hat –
    To cover the seat of reason;
It may look like a rabbit or bat,
Yet this is a lady's hat;
May be ugly, ridiculous, that
    We never remark, 'twould be treason.
This is a lady's hat,
    To cover the seat of reason.

*

These are a lady's shoes,
    Ornaments, curved and bended,
But feet are given to use,
Not merely to show off shoes,
To stand, walk, run if we choose,
    For which these were never intended.
These are a lady's shoes.
    Ornaments, curved and bended.

*

This is a lady's skirt,
    Which limits her locomotion;
Her shape is so smooth-begirt
As to occupy all the skirt,
Of being swift and alert
    She has not the slightest notion;
This is a lady's skirt,
    Which limits her locomotion.

148

MATTHEW SWEENEY

Negations

Style negates soul, you said to me.
I looked at your chic Armani coat,
your purple and blue Von Etzdorf scarf,
and wondered if I still spoke English.
Across the street a white dog barked
at a squawking, one-legged pigeon.
It would die before the day was out
whether or not the dog killed it –
and if the priests at school were right
it was a creature without soul.
It was also a creature without style,
certainly in its final plumage,
but didn't that mean it had a soul
in your mathematical scheme of things?
And weren't you shouting at me
that *you* were the one without soul,
or was this the blatentest of ironies?
And why were you using words like 'soul',
you who espoused the religion of things?
And why 'style', for that matter?
I just smiled and shook my head.
I reminded you about your train.
You kissed me on the cheek and left.
You didn't even glance at the pigeon.

Chosen by Matthew Sweeney

The New Vestments

There lived an old man in the kingdom of Tess,
Who invented a purely original dress;
And when it was perfectly made and complete,
He opened the door, and walked into the street.

By way of a hat, he'd a loaf of Brown Bread,
In the middle of which he inserted his head; –
His Shirt was made up of no end of dead Mice,
The warmth of whose skins was quite fluffy and nice; –
His Drawers were of Rabbit-skins; so were his Shoes;
His Stocking were skins, — but it is not known whose; –
His Waistcoat and Trowsers were made of Pork Chops; –
His Buttons were Jujubes, and Chocolate Drops; –
His Coat was all Pancakes with Jam for a border,
And a girdle of Biscuits to keep it in order;
And he wore over all, as a screen from bad weather,
A Cloak of green Cabbage-leaves stitched all together.

He had walked a short way, when he heard a great noise,
Of all sorts of Beasticles, Birdlings, and Boys; –
And from every long street and dark lane in the town
Beasts, Birdles, and Boys in a tumult rushed down.
Two Cows and a half ate his Cabbage-leaf Cloak; –
Four Apes seized his Girdle, which vanished like smoke; –
Three Kids ate up half of his Pancaky Coat, –
And the tails were devour'd by an ancient He-Goat; –
An army of Dogs in a twinkling tore up his
Pork Waistcoat and Trowsers to give to their Puppies; –

And while they were growling, and mumbling the Chops,
Ten boys prigged the Jujubes and Chocolate Drops. –
He tried to run back to his house, but in vain,
Four Scores of fat Pigs came again and again; –
They rushed out of stables and hovels and doors, –
They tore off his stockings, his shoes, and his drawers; –
And now from the housetops with screechings descend,
Striped, spotted, white, black, and gray Cats without end,
They jumped on his shoulders and knocked off his hat, –
When Crows, Ducks, and Hens made a mincemeat of that; –
They speedily flew at his sleeves in a trice,
And utterly tore up his Shirt of dead Mice; –
They swallowed the last of his Shirt with a squall, –
Whereon he ran home with no clothes on at all.

And he said to himself as he bolted the door,
'I will not wear a similar dress any more,
Any more, any more, any more, never more!'

JANE WEIR

Stomacher*

A level stare at the ordinary as he leaves the house.
The air aches with heat and the narcissi seep, faint apertures
of pheasants eye, in a cut leaded glass, but I don't stir
until I hear the car move off.
I have one hour to bathe, a glass of wine

stains my throat, décolletage going wide and deep.
Time to buff my toes, vanilla my feet. I stayed in
town all winter. In the park we walked Belfast everyday.
The pond went platinum under an ice sun, and when the
seagulls came and shadows bottled green against

the yew we turned back. If there was a hiding place in my shoe
I'd slip you in; I know what you feel like, a bloom of red
that gives warmth to silk. Time rolls like a muff around
my wrist. In a small room a changeling sleeps. The days were
plain and untrimmed till you came. I was a long bodice

partly sewn to a skirt, a hem picking up everything. I have
half an hour left. I partially dress. The bed is a deep breath,
my hair a mound of flothers, combs. Before he left we talked
through the cut and finish. The way it can be darned and
    patched.
I think I said 'yes'. But moments are banners and move on.

And now you are here I am a bodice intact. You place
    yourself,

* Stomacher: The stiffened bib worn over bodice, worn over
the front of a corset.

broad as a scold between the break of my breast bone.
Sweet as a blister I weep, burn to your touch. My belly
    rumbles
for trinkets and nipple kisses. As your hands close, you caress
each steel band, softening bones. No wood block with its
    chastity

of resist, full frontal composition, a stork feeding her young,
can deny me this. My flesh gives, sea visions, tree visions.
And when you go out and he comes in, I never fan an eyelid,
look straight ahead, detached and certain.

KATHERINE MANSFIELD

Chosen by Jane Weir

The Arabian Shawl

'It is cold outside, you will need a coat –
What! This old Arabian shawl!
Bind it about your head and throat,
These steps . . . it is dark . . . my hand . . . you might fall.'

What has happened? What strange, sweet charm
Lingers about the Arabian shawl . . .
Do not tremble so! There can be no harm
In just remembering – that is all.

'I love you so – I will be your wife,'
Here, in the dark of the Terrace wall,
Say it again. Let that other life
Fold us like the Arabian shawl.

'Do you remember?' . . . 'I quite forget,
Some childish foolishness, that is all,
To-night is the first time we have met . . .
Let me take off my Arabian shawl!'

MICHAEL WOODS

Casting Off

The Skerries flinch in the storm
as their rock piles are ramped by the sea.
I knit to the tune of the clock as I rock
through the rock-black, night after night.

The wool I pull from the tangle
of balls in the leather bag lived once,
lagged the legs and hot-tank bodies
of sheep that sleep without dreams.

Shorn, their warmth will froth again
but, like me, they were born to be worn,
our lives twisted together in skeins
that I turn into clothes for the town.

The needles are number eights.
I double knit the three-ply night
into stitches and rows. I know
the patterns as well as the knots

that were veins on the backs of his hands
or the black of the space where his face
used to be, or the giveaway diamond
design of the cable-knit, double-knit

sweater, the one that I sweated myself
from the scores of the pores in my skin,
when time before time I'd wish
that the sea would wash him away.

WILLIAM SHAKESPEARE

Chosen by Michael Woods

Sonnet 52

So am I as the rich, whose blessed key
Can bring him to his sweet up-locked treasure,
The which he will not every hour survey,
For blunting the fine point of seldom pleasure.
Therefore are feasts so solemn and so rare,
Since, seldom coming, in the long year set,
Like stones of worth they thinly placed are,
Or captain jewels in the carcanet.
So is the time that keeps you as my chest,
Or as the wardrobe which the robe doth hide,
To make some special instant special blest,
By new unfolding his imprison'd pride.
   Blessed are you, whose worthiness gives scope,
   Being had, to triumph, being lack'd, to hope.

Elegy

Who'll know then, when they walk by the grave
where your bones will be brittle things – this bone here
that swoops away from your throat, and this,
which perfectly fits the scoop of my palm, and these
which I count with my lips, and your skull,
which blooms on the pillow now, and your fingers,
beautiful in their little rings – that love, which wanders history,
singled you out in your time?

       Love loved you best; lit you
with a flame, like talent, under your skin; let you
move through your days and nights, blessed in your flesh,
blood, hair, as though they were lovely garments
you wore to pleasure the air. Who'll guess, if they read
your stone, or press their thumbs to the scars
of your dates, that were I alive, I would lie on the grass
above your bones till I mirrored your pose, your infinite grace?

Chosen by Carol Ann Duffy

To his Mistress Going to Bed

Come, Madam, come, all rest my powers defie,
Until I labour, I in labour lie.
The foe oft-times having the foe in sight,
Is tir'd with standing though he never fight.
Off with that girdle, like heaven's Zone glistering,
But a far fairer world incompassing.
Unpin that spangled breastplate which you wear,
That th'eyes of busie fooles may be stopt there.
Unlace your self, for that harmonious chyme,
Tells me from you, that now it is bed time.
Off with that happy busk, which I envie,
That still can be, and still can stand so nigh.
Your gown going off, such beautious state reveals,
As when from flowry meads th'hills shadowe steales.
Off with that wyerie Coronet and shew
The haiery Diademe which on you doth grow:
Now off with those shooes, and then safely tread
In this love's hallow'd temple, this soft bed.
In such white robes, heaven's Angels us'd to be
Receavd by men; Thou Angel bringst with thee
A heaven like Mahomets paradice; and though
Ill spirits walk in white, we easly know,
By this these Angels from an evil sprite,
Those set our hairs, but these our flesh upright.
    Licence my roaving hands, and let them go,
Before, behind, between, above, below.
O my America! my new-found-land,
My kingdome, safeliest when with one man man'd,

My Myne of precious stones, My Emperie,
How blest I am in this discovering thee!
To enter in these bonds, is to be free;
Then where my hand is set, my seal shall be.
    Full nakedness! All joyes are due to thee,
As souls unbodied, bodies uncloth'd must be,
To taste whole joyes. Jems which you women use
Are like Atlanta's balls, cast in mens views,
That when a fool's eye lighteth on a Jem,
His earthly soul may covet theirs, not them.
Like pictures, or like books' gay coverings made
For lay-men, are all women thus array'd;
Themselves are mystick books, which only wee
(Whom their imputed grace will dignifie)
Must see reveal'd. Then since that I may know;
As liberally, as to a Midwife, shew
Thy self: cast all, yea, this white lynnen hence,
There is no pennance due to innocence:
    To teach thee, I am naked first; why then
What needst thou have more covering then a man.

Acknowledgements

Faber and Faber would like to thank the following poets for permission to publish their poems: John Agard, Simon Armitage; Colette Bryce; Nina Cassian; Kate Clanchy; Fred D'Aguiar; Julia Darling; Imtiaz Dharker; Maura Dooley; Nick Drake; Carol Ann Duffy, Douglas Dunn; Vicki Feaver; Philip Gross, Lavinia Greenlaw; David Hart, David Harsent; Jackie Kay; Christopher Logue; Ian McMillan, Dorothy Molloy; Andrew Motion; Paul Muldoon; Grace Nichols; Alice Oswald; Craig Raine; Jo Shapcott; Clare Shaw; Owen Sheers; Alicia Stubbersfield; Matthew Sweeney; Jane Weir; and Michael Woods.

The publishers would also like to thank the following poets, translators and literary representatives, whose work is reprinted in this edition: Moniza Alvi: 'The Sari', from *Carrying My Wife* (Bloodaxe Books, 2000); Associated University Presses: 'This Is a Lady's Hat', from *The Later Poetry of Charlotte Perkins Gilman*, edited by Denise D. Knight (Associated University Presses, 1996); Bloodaxe Books: 'Nothing but Curves', from *Cusan Dyn Dall/Blind Man's Kiss* by Menna Elfyn (Bloodaxe Books, 2001); and 'Remapping the Border', from *Sunny Side Plucked: New and Selected Poems* by Rita Ann Higgins (Bloodaxe Books, 1996); Geoffrey Bownas and Anthony Thwaite: 'Poem by a Frontier Guard' (Anonymous), from *The Penguin Book of Japanese Verse*, edited and translated by Geoffrey Bownas and Anthony Thwaite (Penguin Books, 1964; 1998), © Geoffrey Bownas and Anthony Thwaite, 1964, 1998; Carcanet Press: 'In Her Green Dress, She is', from *A Colour for Solitude* by Sujata Bhatt (Carcanet Press, 2002); 'Amber', from *Five Fields* by Gillian Clarke (Carcanet Press, 1998); 'Waiting for the Day', from *Selected Poems* by Roger Garfitt (Carcanet Press, 2000); 'Nineteen Thirties Suit', from *Walking the Animals* by Carola Luther (Carcanet Press, 2004); 'We Shall Not Escape Hell' by Marina

Tsvetaeva, translated by Elaine Feinstein, from *Collected Poems and Translations* by Elaine Feinstein (Carcanet Press, 2002); Linda Chase: 'My Father Had Two Coats', from Young Men Dancing (Smith/Doorstop Books, 1994); Anthony Conran: 'Song to a Child' (Anonymous) and 'The Shirt of a Lad' (Anonymous), from *The Penguin Book of Welsh Verse*, edited and translated by Anthony Conran (Penguin Books, 1967); Adam Czerniawski: 'Laments: VII', from *Treny: The Laments of Kochanowski* by Jan Kochanowski, translated by Adam Czerniawski (European Humanities Research Centre, 2001); Carol Ann Duffy; 'Warming Her Pearls', from *Selling Manhattan* (Anvil Press Poetry, 1987); Faber and Faber: 'The Large Cool Store', from *Philip Larkin: Collected Poems* (Faber and Faber, 1988); 'The Blue Jacket', from *The Turn of the Day* by Marion Angus (Faber and Faber, 1931); 'Disillusionment of Ten o'Clock', from *Selected Poems of Wallace Stevens* (Faber and Faber, 1965); Famous Music Corporation: 'Buttons and Bows' (Words and Music by Jay Livingston and Ray Evans), from the film The Paleface (1948). Rights administisistered by BMG Music Publishing International, Bedford House, 69–79 Fulham High Street, London SW6 3JW. All Rights Reserved. Farrar, Straus and Giroux: 'Exchanging Hats', from *The Complete Poems 1927–1979* by Elizabeth Bishop (Farrar, Straus and Giroux, 1979), © 1979, 1983 by Alice Helen Methfessel; Ann Gray: 'Twice', from *Painting Skin* (Fatchance Press, 1995); Harvard University Press: 'I started Early – Took my Dog', from *The Complete Poems of Emily Dickinson*, edited by Thomas H. Johnson (Harvard University Press, 1955); Alice Kavounas: 'The Man in the Lacoste Shirt', from *The Invited* (Sinclair-Stevenson, 1995); Hamish MacGibbon: 'My Hat', from *The Collected Poems of Stevie Smith* (Penguin Modern Classics, 1985); Paula Meehan: 'Valentine', published in *The Irish Times* (2003); Sarah Maguire: 'The Invisible Mender' from *The Invisible Mender* (Jonathan Cape, 1997); Julie O'Callaghan: 'Well-Heeled', from *What's What* (Bloodaxe Books, 1991); Dennis O'Driscoll: 'Success Story', from *Quality Time* (Anvil Press Poetry, 1997); Pan Macmillan: 'Cousin Coat', from *Cousin Coat: Selected Poems 1976–2001* by Sean O'Brien (Picador, 2002); Peterloo Poets and the author: 'Rag Trade', from *A Watching Brief* by U. A. Fanthorpe (Peterloo Poets, 1987); The Peters Fraser and

Index of Poets